WILLIAMS-SONOMA

FRUIT DESSERT

RECIPES AND TEXT
CAROLYN BETH WEIL

GENERAL EDITOR
CHUCK WILLIAMS

PHOTOGRAPHS
MAREN CARUSO

SIMON & SCHUSTER • **SOURCE**

NEW YORK • LONDON • TORONTO • SYDNEY

CONTENTS

THE CLASSICS

QUICK AND SIMPLE

CRISPS AND COBBLERS

PIES AND TARTS

PUDDINGS AND FROZEN DESSERTS

SPECIAL OCCASIONS

INTRODUCTION

A dessert that takes advantage of fresh fruit is the most simple, wholesome, and enjoyable way to end a meal, and in these pages you will find sweet fruit dishes for every season. In summer, peaches, nectarines, and ripe berries lend themselves to making pies, cobblers, and ice creams. Fall and winter specialties such as an apple crisp or a rustic pandowdy pie made with dried apricots, raisins, and cinnamon are always welcome around the holidays. And in spring, ripe strawberries make their way into everything from a layer cake to a decadent ice cream.

If you have not yet mastered the technique for making flaky pie crust, working with filo dough, or whipping up a stable meringue, you will find assistance in the basics section at the back of the book. Additional tips in the sidebars and the glossary will further your knowledge of baking and help you select and make the most of fruit at its peak of ripeness so that each dessert you try is a great success. I welcome you to enjoy these favorite recipes and to share them with your friends and family.

THE CLASSICS

Each time-honored dessert in this chapter features the full flavor of ripe fruit. Sweet red strawberries folded into whipped cream make the perfect complement to a moist yellow sponge cake, while the simple goodness of spiced apples emerges under a crisp topping. And a custard tart decorated with a colorful array of seasonal fruits is a wonderful addition to any meal.

APPLE CRISP

CUTTING IN BUTTER

Cutting butter into flour gives pie crusts, biscuits, and cobbler toppings their trademark flakiness, and it gives crisp and crumble toppings their distinctive crumbly character. To cut in butter, use a pastry blender *(above)* or 2 knives to cut and toss the butter until the mixture resembles a coarse meal, with the largest pieces of butter the size of small peas. The butter should remain in small but discrete pieces. It's important to start with cold butter and to work quickly so that the butter doesn't soften and melt.

Place an oven rack in the lower third of the oven and preheat to 350°F (180°C). Lightly grease a 12-inch (30-cm) oval or 9-by-13- inch (23-by-33-cm) rectangular baking dish with a 2-qt (2-l) capacity.

To make the topping, in a bowl, stir together the flour, oats, brown sugar, salt, and cinnamon. Using a pastry blender or two knives, quickly cut or rub the butter into the flour mixture until it is crumbly. Add the walnuts and toss to mix. Cover and refrigerate while you prepare the filling.

To make the filling, in a small bowl, stir together the granulated sugar, salt, nutmeg, and cinnamon. Place the apple slices in a large bowl, sprinkle with the sugar mixture, and toss to distribute evenly. Spread the apple mixture in the prepared baking dish. Sprinkle the topping evenly over the apples.

Bake until the topping is crisp and golden brown and the apples are tender when pierced with the tip of a knife, about 50 minutes. Serve warm.

Serving Tip: Accompany with a scoop of good-quality ice cream or a dollop of Sweetened Whipped Cream (page 17).

MAKES 8 SERVINGS

FOR THE CRISP TOPPING:

½ cup (2½ oz/75 g) unbleached all-purpose (plain) flour

1 cup (3 oz/90 g) old-fashioned or quick-cooking rolled oats

½ cup (3½ oz/105 g) firmly packed brown sugar

¼ teaspoon salt

½ teaspoon ground cinnamon

½ cup (4 oz/125 g) cold unsalted butter, cut into ¼-inch (6-mm) cubes, plus extra for greasing

½ cup (2 oz/60 g) walnuts, finely chopped

FOR THE APPLE FILLING:

¾ cup (6 oz/185 g) granulated sugar

Pinch of salt

¼ teaspoon freshly grated nutmeg

½ teaspoon ground cinnamon

6 medium, tart apples such as pippin and Granny Smith, peeled, halved, cored, and sliced ¼ inch (6 mm) thick (about 6 cups/1½ lb/750 g)

LEMON MERINGUE PIE

One rolled-out Basic Pie Dough round (page 110)

FOR THE LEMON FILLING:

1¼ cups (10 oz/315 g) sugar

3 tablespoons cornstarch (cornflour)

4 large whole eggs, plus 4 large egg yolks

2 tablespoons finely grated lemon zest

1 cup (8 fl oz/250 ml) fresh lemon juice (about 7 large lemons)

4 tablespoons (2 oz/60 g) unsalted butter, thinly sliced

Meringue Topping *(far right)*, made just before using

Fold the dough round in half and transfer to a 9-inch (23-cm) pie pan or dish. Unfold and ease into the pan without stretching it, patting it firmly into the bottom and up the sides. Trim the edge of the dough, leaving ¾ inch (2 cm) of overhang. Fold the overhang under itself and pinch to create a high edge on the pan's rim. Flute the edge decoratively (page 108). Refrigerate or freeze until firm, about 30 minutes. Place an oven rack in the lower third of the oven and preheat to 375°F (190°C).

Line the pie shell with aluminum foil and cover the bottom with pie weights. Bake for 25 minutes. When the dough looks firm and dry, remove the weights and foil and continue baking until golden, 10–15 minutes more. Transfer to a wire rack to cool.

To make the filling, in a bowl, whisk together the sugar and cornstarch. Add the whole eggs and egg yolks and whisk until pale yellow. Whisk in the lemon zest and juice, then the butter. Transfer to a saucepan and cook over medium heat, stirring constantly, until the mixture begins to bubble and is very thick, about 10 minutes. Pour the mixture into a bowl through a medium-mesh sieve. Spread the filling evenly in the baked crust. Cover with plastic wrap, pressing the wrap directly onto the surface. Refrigerate until well chilled and set, 3–4 hours.

Preheat the oven to 375°F (190°C). Make the topping *(right)*. Heap the topping onto the filling and spread it to the edges of the crust, using a spatula or the back of a spoon to make large swirls. Bake the pie until the meringue is an even light gold, 15–18 minutes. Transfer to a rack and let stand until cool, 20 minutes or longer.

To serve, cut into wedges using a thin, sharp knife dipped into hot water. The pie is best eaten the day it is baked, but it can be stored in the refrigerator, well wrapped, for 2–3 days.

MAKE ONE 9-INCH (23-CM) PIE, OR 8 SERVINGS

MERINGUE TOPPING

In a saucepan, whisk together 1 tablespoon cornstarch (cornflour) and ¼ cup (2 fl oz/60 ml) water. Cook over medium heat, stirring constantly, until thick, about 2 minutes. Let cool. In a bowl, using an electric mixer on high speed, whip 4 large egg whites and ½ teaspoon cream of tartar until foamy. Reduce the speed to medium and whip while sprinkling in ½ cup (4 oz/125 g) sugar. Return to high speed and whip until the whites form a ribbon that folds back on itself when the beater is raised. Stir in the cornstarch mixture and beat on high speed until shiny and soft peaks form, 2–3 minutes.

CLASSIC FRUIT TART

Fold the dough round in half and transfer to a 9½-inch (24-cm) tart pan with removable bottom. Unfold and ease into the pan, patting it firmly into the bottom and sides. Trim off any excess dough. Refrigerate or freeze the tart shell for at least 30 minutes.

Preheat the oven to 375°F (190°C). Line the tart shell with foil and cover the bottom with pie weights. Bake until the dough is set and dry, about 25 minutes. Remove the weights and foil and continue baking until the crust is golden, about 10 minutes more. Let cool.

To make the pastry cream, in a nonreactive saucepan over medium heat, heat the milk until tiny bubbles start to appear. Remove from the heat. In a bowl, whisk together the egg yolks and sugar until pale yellow. Add the cornstarch and salt and whisk well. Gradually pour half of the hot milk into the yolk mixture while whisking constantly to avoid curdling the yolks. Whisk in the remaining milk and return the mixture to the saucepan. Cook over medium heat, whisking constantly, until the mixture thickens to a puddinglike consistency, 8–10 minutes. (Do not let it boil.) Scrape into a bowl and whisk in the vanilla. Cover with plastic wrap. Refrigerate until chilled, 2–3 hours.

To assemble the tart, stir the chilled pastry cream until smooth. Spoon the pastry cream into the bottom of the cooled tart shell and spread evenly. Overlap the mango slices in a ring around the rim of the tart. Arrange the strawberry halves, cut side down, as a second ring inside the first, and arrange the raspberries in a third ring. Overlap the kiwifruit slices in a fourth concentric ring, and fill the hole at the center with the blueberries.

In a saucepan over low heat, heat the apricot jam until it liquefies. Strain into a small bowl. Using a pastry brush, brush the fruit with a thin coating of the jam. Serve the tart at room temperature.

MAKES ONE 9½-INCH (24-CM) TART, OR 8 SERVINGS

HULLING STRAWBERRIES

When selecting strawberries, which reach their peak in late spring and early summer, look for deep-red berries with a strong strawberry scent. Avoid large berries with white shoulders under the green leaves; they are usually woody and lack flavor. To prepare the berries for use, remove the leaves, rinse the fruit gently, and pat dry with a paper towel. With a small, sharp knife, remove the stem and the white core, if there is one, in the center of the berry (this process is called "hulling"). Then cut as directed.

One rolled-out Basic Tart Dough round (page 110)

FOR THE PASTRY CREAM:

1½ cups (12 fl oz/375 ml) whole milk

4 large egg yolks

⅓ cup (3 oz/90 g) sugar

3 tablespoons cornstarch (cornflour)

⅛ teaspoon salt

1 teaspoon vanilla extract (essence)

FOR THE FRUIT TOPPING:

1 mango, peeled (page 35) and cut into slices ¼ inch (6 mm) thick

2 cups (8 oz/250 g) strawberries, hulled *(far left)* and halved lengthwise

1 cup (4 oz/125 g) raspberries

2 or 3 kiwifruits, peeled, halved lengthwise, and cut crosswise into slices ¼ inch (6 mm) thick

½ cup (2 oz/60 g) blueberries

⅓ cup (3½ oz/105 g) apricot jam

STRAWBERRIES-AND-CREAM CAKE

One 8-inch (20-cm) round Yellow Sponge Cake (page 109)

About 6 cups (1½ lb/ 750 g) strawberries

FOR THE SWEETENED WHIPPED CREAM:

2 cups (16 fl oz/500 ml) cold heavy (double) cream

2 teaspoons vanilla extract (essence)

2 tablespoons confectioners' (icing) sugar

Prepare the cake and allow to cool completely. Using a serrated knife, cut the cake horizontally into 3 equal layers (page 106).

Reserve 8 attractive strawberries of uniform size for garnishing. Hull the remaining berries (page 14) and slice lengthwise. You should have about 2 cups.

To make the whipped cream, in a deep bowl, combine the cream, vanilla, and sugar. Using a wire whisk or electric beater on medium speed, beat until soft peaks form when the whisk is lifted, 6–8 minutes.

Spoon about one-fourth of the whipped cream on top of the bottom cake layer and spread evenly. Cover with half of the sliced strawberries. Place the second cake layer on top of the berries and spread with one-third of the remaining whipped cream and all of the remaining sliced strawberries. Place the third cake layer on top.

Using the wire whisk, continue to beat the remaining cream until medium peaks form when the whisk is lifted. Use the remaining whipped cream to frost the top and sides of the cake. Decorate the top of the cake with the 8 reserved strawberries.

Make-Ahead Tip: It's best to bake the cake a couple of hours ahead, then refrigerate it (away from strong odors) before assembling. Once assembled, let the cake come to room temperature for 20 minutes before serving.

MAKES ONE 9-INCH (23-CM) CAKE, OR 10–12 SERVINGS

WHIPPING CREAM

Heavy (double) cream is best whipped when it is very cold. If your kitchen is warm, chill the bowl and beaters (or whisk) as well. Confectioners' (icing) sugar dissolves into the cream more readily than granulated, but either type may be used. For topping a pie or crumble, whip the cream just until soft, slumping peaks form when the whisk is lifted. Cream that is intended for folding into another mixture or for frosting a cake is usually whipped until more pointed medium peaks form *(above)*. To rescue over-whipped cream with a chunky texture, fold in liquid cream 1 tablespoon at a time.

PINEAPPLE UPSIDE-DOWN CAKE

PEELING PINEAPPLE

A ripe pineapple is fragrant and golden and gives slightly when pressed. Its thick skin and bumpy "eyes" must be cut away before the pineapple is eaten. Slice off the top and bottom with crosswise cuts. Stand the fruit upright and, using a sharp knife, slice off the skin. Place the pineapple on its side and, following the spiral pattern of eyes that starts at the top of the pineapple and ends at the bottom, cut a shallow, wedge-shaped furrow to remove the eyes. The pineapple may now be sliced crosswise and the hard center core cut out from each slice.

Preheat the oven to 350°F (180°C). Lightly coat a 9-inch (23-cm) round cake pan with vegetable oil spray.

Cut the pineapple crosswise into slices ½ inch (12 mm) thick. With a paring knife or small cookie cutter, remove the core from each slice. Cut the pineapple rounds into half-moons and set aside.

In a saucepan over medium heat, melt the butter. Add the brown sugar and stir until small bubbles appear, 2–3 minutes. Remove the sugar mixture from the heat and pour into the pan. Arrange 7–8 pineapple halves in the pan in a circular pattern. Set aside.

To make the cake, in a bowl, mix together the flour, baking powder, salt, and nutmeg. Set aside. In another bowl, whisk the eggs with the vanilla. Set aside. In a stand mixer fitted with the paddle attachment, beat the butter until pale and fluffy. Gradually add the granulated sugar and beat for 2–3 minutes longer. Slowly add the egg mixture, beating after each addition. Spoon half of the flour mixture into the butter mixture, stir, add half of the milk, and stir again. Add the remaining flour, stir, and add the remaining milk. Continue stirring, scraping down the bowl as needed, until the batter is completely smooth. Do not overmix.

Pour the batter on top of the pineapple slices in the prepared pan, spreading it evenly. Bake until the top of the cake is lightly golden and the center springs back when touched, 35–45 minutes. Let the cake cool in the pan on a wire rack for 5–10 minutes, then turn out onto a platter and scrape the remaining juices over the top of cake. Let cool slightly and serve warm.

MAKES ONE 9-INCH (23-CM) CAKE, OR 8 SERVINGS

Variation Note: If desired, leave the pineapple rounds whole and do not overlap them in the pan. Place a poached cherry in the center of each round.

Vegetable oil spray

½ fresh pineapple, peeled *(far left)*

¼ cup (2 oz/60 g) unsalted butter

¾ cup (6 oz/185 g) firmly packed brown sugar

FOR THE CAKE:

1¾ cups (9 oz/280 g) unbleached all-purpose (plain) flour

1 teaspoon baking powder

¼ teaspoon salt

⅛ teaspoon freshly grated nutmeg

2 large eggs

2 teaspoons vanilla extract (essence)

¾ cup (6 oz/185 g) unsalted butter, at room temperature

1 cup (8 oz/250 g) granulated sugar

½ cup (4 fl oz/125 ml) whole milk

PEARS POACHED IN RED WINE

4 firm but ripe Bosc
pears of uniform size

1 bottle (24 fl oz/750 ml)
fruity red wine such as
Merlot or Zinfandel

¾ cup (6 oz/185 g) sugar

1 strip lemon zest,
2 inches (5 cm) long
and 1 inch (2.5 cm) wide

1 cinnamon stick,
2–3 inches (5–7.5 cm) long

2 whole cloves

2 tablespoons unsalted
butter, at room
temperature

Peel the pears, leaving the stems in place. Working from the blossom (bottom) end, and using a melon baller or apple corer, remove the core from each pear, stopping within 1 inch (2.5 cm) of the stem end. Remove a thin slice from bottom of each pear so that it will stand upright.

Select a deep saucepan with a tight-fitting lid just large enough to accommodate the pears. In the saucepan, combine the wine, sugar, lemon zest, cinnamon stick, and cloves and stir to dissolve the sugar. Add the pears, standing them close to one another in the pan. If the pears are not covered by the wine, add just enough water to cover them completely.

Bring the mixture to a boil over medium heat, then reduce the heat to maintain a slow, gentle simmer. Poach, uncovered, until the pears are tender when pierced with a skewer or cake tester, 20–30 minutes, depending on the firmness of the pear. Using a slotted spoon, carefully remove the pears from the liquid. Let cool to room temperature and cover with plastic wrap.

Return the wine mixture to medium heat and simmer until it is reduced to ¾ cup (6 fl oz/180 ml) and has the consistency of a thick syrup, 40–50 minutes. (The pears and syrup may be prepared to this point up to 2 days in advance and stored in the refrigerator. The pears should be brought to room temperature and the syrup reheated before serving.)

To serve, add the butter to the hot syrup and swirl the mixture in the pan until the butter is melted. Divide the pears among individual shallow dessert bowls or deep plates. Pour an equal amount of the sauce over each pear and serve immediately.

MAKES 4 SERVINGS

POACHING

Poaching, or cooking in liquid at a temperature just below the boiling point, is a gentle method that works well for delicate foods like fruit. Here, pears are cooked in wine, and the poaching liquid is then reduced to make a sauce. Heating the pears along with the wine, rather than adding them to an already-simmering mixture, causes the flavor of the fruit to infuse the syrupy liquid. Once the liquid comes to a boil, reduce the heat as needed to maintain a gentle simmer, with large bubbles slowly breaking the surface.

CHERRY CLAFOUTI

Preheat the oven to 425°F (220°C). Generously grease a 12-inch (30-cm) oval or 9-by-13 inch (23-by-33-cm) rectangular baking dish with a 2 qt (2-l) capacity with the butter. Dust with the 2 tablespoons granulated sugar. Spread the cherries in an even layer in the dish.

In a blender, combine the ½ cup granulated sugar, eggs, milk, Kirsch, vanilla, zest, and salt. Blend until smooth, about 1 minute. Add the flour and ground almonds and blend until smooth, about 1 minute. Scrape down the sides of the blender and blend for 30 seconds more. Pour the mixture into the pan over the cherries and spread evenly.

Bake until the clafouti's edges are puffed and golden, the center is firm, and a skewer inserted in the middle comes out clean, 40–45 minutes. Let cool on a wire rack for about 30 minutes.

Using a fine-mesh sieve, dust the surface with confectioners' sugar. Serve warm or at room temperature.

Note: In the French countryside, this summertime favorite is typically made with whole unpitted cherries, which prevents the cherry juice from bleeding into the batter as it bakes. You may choose to use whole cherries here, but be sure to alert diners to the presence of the pits.

MAKES 8 SERVINGS

GRINDING ALMONDS

Almonds and stone fruits such as cherries, whose pits have an almondlike flavor, have a natural affinity. Look for finely ground almonds, or almond flour, at specialty markets, or grind whole nuts yourself. Choose raw or blanched untoasted almonds. About ¾ cup (3½ oz/105 g) whole almonds will be needed to yield ½ cup (2 oz/60 g) ground nuts. Almonds are best ground in a nut grinder, although a food processor will also work. Use short pulses and be sure not to grind the almonds for too long, or you'll end up extracting the nut oils and producing almond butter.

1–2 tablespoons unsalted butter, at room temperature

½ cup (4 oz/125 g) plus 2 tablespoons granulated sugar

3 cups (1 lb/500 g) fresh or frozen cherries, pitted (see Note)

4 large eggs

1½ cups (12 fl oz/375 ml) whole milk

2 tablespoons Kirsch or other cherry brandy (page 93)

2 teaspoons vanilla extract (essence)

½ teaspoon finely grated lemon zest

¼ teaspoon salt

¾ cup (4 oz/125 g) unbleached all-purpose (plain) flour

½ cup (2 oz/60 g) finely ground almonds *(far left)*

Confectioners' (icing) sugar for dusting

MIXED BERRY CHEESECAKE

FOR THE CRUST:

Vegetable oil spray

1½ cups (4½ oz/140 g) graham cracker crumbs

2 tablespoons sugar

½ teaspoon ground cinnamon

4 tablespoons (2 oz/60 g) unsalted butter, melted

FOR THE FILLING:

1 lb (500 g) cream cheese (see Note)

⅔ cup (5 oz/155 g) sugar

2 large eggs

1 cup (8 fl oz/250 ml) sour cream

½ teaspoon vanilla extract (essence)

1 cup (4 oz/125 g) raspberries

1 cup (4 oz/125 g) blueberries

¼ cup (3 oz/90 g) red currant jelly (optional)

Place an oven rack in the lower third of the oven and preheat to 325°F (165°C). To make the crust, coat an 8-inch (20-cm) spring-form pan with vegetable oil spray. In a bowl, combine the graham cracker crumbs, sugar, and cinnamon. Stir in the melted butter until the crumbs are evenly moistened. Press the crumb mixture firmly and evenly into the pan, bringing it 2–3 inches (5–7.5 cm) up the sides.

To make the filling, in a bowl, using an electric mixer on medium speed, beat the cream cheese until smooth. Add the sugar and continue beating until combined. Add the eggs one at a time and mix well; do not overbeat. Add the sour cream and vanilla, then beat until smooth. Pour the mixture into the prepared crust.

Bake the cheesecake for 1 hour. Turn off the oven and let the cheesecake remain in the warm oven, without opening the door, for 1 hour longer to cool slowly (this will help prevent it from cracking). Let the cake cool completely on a wire rack before refrigerating, then chill for at least 3 hours or up to overnight.

Remove the cheesecake from the refrigerator and release the pan sides. If necessary, run a small knife around the edge to release the cake before lifting the pan sides away from the cake.

Arrange the berries in a circular pattern (or as you wish) on top of the cheesecake. Up to an hour before serving, in a small saucepan over low heat, heat the currant jelly until it liquefies. Using a pastry brush, gently brush the jelly on the berries, giving the cake a glossy finish. (The jelly will soften and drip if the cheesecake is stored too long.) Serve the cheesecake at room temperature, cut into neat wedges.

Note: Do not use nonfat or low-fat cream cheese for this recipe.

MAKES ONE 8-INCH (20-CM) CAKE, OR 10 SERVINGS

SPRINGFORM PANS

A springform pan has removable sides that are secured with a clasp, a design that allows cakes baked in it to be removed easily. After the cake is baked, the clasp is opened and the pan sides are released, freeing the cake. You can serve the cake directly from the bottom of the pan, or you can run a long, thin spatula under the cake to loosen it and then slide it onto a flat serving platter.

QUICK AND SIMPLE

There are times when you'd like a sweet finish to dinner, but the prospect of making dessert is daunting. These quick and simple recipes are perfect for those occasions. Apples baked in the oven alongside a roasting chicken are an ideal ending for an autumn meal, while fresh melon and mint combine to make a lightning-quick dessert on a summer night.

MELON BALLS WITH FRESH MINT

Cut the melons in half and use a spoon to remove the seeds. Using a melon baller, scoop the melon flesh into balls, gently tapping the handle of the utensil on the edge of a bowl to release the fruit. You should have about 6 cups (2¼ lb/1.1 kg) in all.

Place the melon balls in a large bowl and sprinkle with the salt and sugar to taste.

Stack the mint leaves on top of one another, roll lengthwise into a cigar shape, and slice crosswise as thinly as possible to make a chiffonade. Sprinkle the mint chiffonade over the melon balls and stir to mix.

Spoon the melon balls into 6 goblets and serve cool, but not cold.

MAKES 6 SERVINGS

2–3 ripe melons such as cantaloupe, honeydew, Crenshaw, casaba, or watermelon *(far left)*

Pinch of salt

1–2 tablespoons sugar

12 fresh mint leaves

MELON VARIETIES

Nothing surpasses the fragrant, sweet flavor of a ripe melon, but finding a good one can be tricky. Most melons are at their best from early summer to mid-fall. For a pretty presentation of this dessert, use a variety of melons in an array of colors. Orange-fleshed cantaloupe and pale green honeydew should have a strong, sweet aroma; as they ripen they become softer and the blossom ends give slightly when pressed. Juicy, red-fleshed watermelons should sound hollow when thumped, and the white patch on one side should be small.

BAKED APPLES

4 firm sweet-tart apples
(far right)

¼ cup (1½ oz/45 g) dried
currants or raisins

¼ cup (1 oz/30 g) chopped
walnuts

4 cinnamon sticks

4 tablespoons (2 oz/60 g)
firmly packed brown sugar

¼ cup (3 fl oz/85 ml) pure
maple syrup

Heavy (double) cream or
good-quality vanilla ice
cream for serving

Preheat the oven to 350°F (180°C).

With an apple corer, core the apples, then peel the skin from the top third of each apple. If necessary, cut a thin slice off the blossom (bottom) end of each apple so that it will stand upright.

Place the apples 1 inch (2.5 cm) apart in a baking dish with a lid. In a small bowl, combine the currants and walnuts. Insert a cinnamon stick in the hollow center of each apple, then stuff each apple with about 1 tablespoon of the currant-walnut mixture. Pat 1 tablespoon brown sugar on top of each apple. Drizzle maple syrup evenly over each apple.

Cover the baking dish and bake the apples, basting them occasionally with their juices, until they are tender when pierced with a skewer or small knife, 1–1½ hours. The timing will depend on the size of the apples.

Serve the apples warm with a drizzle of cream or a scoop of vanilla ice cream.

MAKES 4 SERVINGS

APPLES FOR BAKING

The best apples for baking have a full, slightly tart flavor and hold their shape in the intense heat of the oven. When selecting apples for baking, keep in mind that underripe fruits will bake up rubbery and result in a watery dessert, while old apples will be mushy and tasteless. Some varieties begin to ripen in mid- or late summer, but the best baking apples come into season in autumn. Braeburn, Jonathan, Newtown pippin, Winesap, and Empire are all good choices. Visit your local farmers' markets to find regional varieties.

RASPBERRY RHUBARB FOOL

Prepare an ice bath by partially filling a sink or large bowl with ice water. In a saucepan over medium heat, combine the rhubarb, ½ cup (4 fl oz/125 ml) water, granulated sugar, and salt. Cook, stirring occasionally, until the rhubarb is soft, 10–15 minutes. Remove from the heat and pour into a large bowl. Set the bowl in the ice bath to cool, stirring occasionally. Once the mixture has come to room temperature, place it in the refrigerator to chill, about 1 hour.

Put the raspberry purée in a large bowl and stir in the cream and confectioners' sugar. Using an electric mixer on medium speed, beat until soft peaks form when the beater is lifted.

Spoon half of the rhubarb into 4 goblets or dessert cups. Layer half of the raspberry cream on top of the rhubarb. Spoon the remaining rhubarb on top of the cream, then top with the remaining raspberry cream. Place in the refrigerator for 1 hour to chill, and serve cold.

Note: A "fool" is a traditional English dessert, usually made from puréed fruit combined with whipped cream.

Serving Tip: To serve this dessert in tall, narrow glasses, put the rhubarb and the raspberry cream in separate pastry bags and pipe into the glasses using a large, round tip.

MAKES 4 SERVINGS

4 or 5 stalks rhubarb (about 1 lb/500 g), trimmed and cut into ⅛-inch (3-mm) pieces

¾ cup (6 oz/185 g) granulated sugar

Pinch of salt

1 cup (8 oz/250 ml) Raspberry Purée (page 109)

1½ cups (12 fl oz/ 375 ml) heavy (double) cream, preferably not ultrapasteurized

½ cup (2 oz/60 g) confectioners' (icing) sugar

ABOUT RHUBARB
Rhubarb grows in thick, celerylike stalks and has a tart, fruity flavor. Field rhubarb is available in summer and is a bright cherry red. Its flavor is more pronounced than that of hot-house rhubarb, which is a brilliant pink and is usually available year-round. Select crisp, unblemished, brightly colored stalks. To avoid a stringy filling, always slice the rhubarb no thicker than ½ inch (12 mm). For the purposes of this recipe, it is chopped even finer.

TROPICAL FRUIT PARFAIT

1 large ripe mango, peeled and pitted *(far right)*

1 fresh papaya, peeled, halved, and seeded

¼ fresh pineapple, peeled, sliced ¼ inch (6 mm) thick, and cored (page 18)

1 kiwifruit, peeled

Zest and juice of 1 lime

1 tablespoon sugar, plus more as needed

Pinch of salt

1 tablespoon Cointreau or rum

1 pint (16 fl oz/500 ml) Coconut Ice Cream (page 111) or good-quality purchased coconut ice cream or sorbet

Cut the mango, papaya, pineapple, and kiwifruit into ¼-inch (6-mm) cubes. In a bowl, combine the fruit, lime zest and juice, the 1 tablespoon sugar, the salt, and the Cointreau. Stir, taste, and add additional sugar if needed. Cover and refrigerate until cold, about 1 hour.

Remove the ice cream from the freezer to soften until it can be easily scooped. Divide half of the fruit among 6 parfait or pilsner glasses. Add 1 medium scoop of ice cream to each glass and carefully press into the fruit. Divide the remaining fruit among the glasses, spooning it over the ice cream. Top each glass with one more scoop of ice cream. Place the parfaits in the freezer for up to 2 hours before serving.

Serving Tip: If this dessert is left in the freezer for more than 2 hours, the fruit will become too hard.

MAKES 6 SERVINGS

PREPARING MANGO
Ripe mangoes give slightly when pressed and are fragrant at the stem end. Depending on the variety, they can range in color from green to various shades of orange, yellow, and red. When cutting a mango, the goal is to remove as much flesh as possible from both sides of the wide, flat pit. Peel the fruit with a vegetable peeler or small, sharp knife, then stand it on one narrow side with the stem pointing toward you. Slice down on one side of the stem, just grazing the pit. Repeat on the other side. Trim the remaining flesh away from the pit.

WARM BERRY COMPOTE

In a large, nonreactive sauté pan over medium heat, combine ¼ cup (2 fl oz/60 ml) water and the sugar and bring to a boil, stirring to dissolve the sugar. Cook for 2 minutes, then add the strawberries, blueberries, blackberries, lemon juice, and salt. Return to a boil, add the butter, and swirl the mixture in the pan until the butter melts.

Spoon the berries along with the sauce onto warmed dessert plates and place a small scoop of vanilla ice cream in the center of each plate. Serve immediately.

MAKES 4 SERVINGS

½ cup (4 oz/125 g) sugar

2 cups (8 oz/250 g) strawberries, hulled (page 14) and quartered

1 cup (4 oz/125 g) blueberries

1 cup (4 oz/125 g) blackberries

2 teaspoons fresh lemon juice

Pinch of salt

¼ cup (2 oz/60 g) unsalted butter at room temperature, cut into ¼-inch (6-mm) cubes

Good-quality vanilla ice cream for serving

HANDLING BERRIES

Although some berries can be found in the market year-round, most taste best in spring and summer, when they are in season. Select plump berries with a deep color and bright flavor. Before storing berries, sort them to remove any with blemishes or mold. Spread them in a single layer on a paper towel–lined plate or baking sheet and refrigerate until ready to use. Just before using the berries, quickly rinse them under cold running water and then gently pat them dry. Do not allow berries to soak in water, as they will absorb moisture and turn mushy.

COCONUT CAKE WITH MANGO

FOR THE COCONUT CAKE:

Vegetable oil spray

1½ cups (7½ oz/235 g) unbleached all-purpose (plain) flour, plus extra for dusting

1½ teaspoons baking powder

½ teaspoon salt

½ cup (4 oz/125 g) unsalted butter, at room temperature

¾ cups (6 oz/185 g) sugar

2 large eggs

1½ teaspoons coconut extract (essence)

½ teaspoon vanilla extract (essence)

½ cup (4 fl oz/125 ml) whole milk

1 cup (4 oz/125 g) sweetened shredded coconut, lightly toasted and cooled (far right)

2 large ripe mangoes, peeled, pitted, and cut into ¼-inch (6-mm) cubes (page 35)

2 teaspoons fresh lime juice

1–2 tablespoons sugar

Position a rack in the lower third of the oven and preheat to 325°F (165°C). Coat a 5-by-9-by-4-inch (13-by-23-by-10-cm) loaf pan with vegetable oil spray. Dust the pan with flour, then tap out any excess.

To make the cake, sift together the flour, baking powder, and salt into a bowl and set aside. In a stand mixer fitted with the paddle attachment, beat the butter on medium speed until pale and fluffy. Add the sugar and beat well. Add the eggs one at a time, beating well after each addition. Add the coconut and vanilla extracts. Beat in half the flour mixture, then half the milk, and repeat to add the remaining flour and milk. Reserve 1 tablespoon of the shredded coconut for garnish and stir in the remainder.

Scrape the batter into the prepared pan. Bake until the top is golden and the center is firm to the touch, 55–60 minutes. Let cool in the pan on a wire rack for 20–30 minutes, then turn out of the pan.

In a large bowl, sprinkle the mango cubes with the lime juice and sugar to taste and toss to distribute evenly. Place a slice of warm or room-temperature coconut cake on each dessert plate. Spoon the mango mixture over each slice of cake and garnish with the reserved coconut. Serve immediately.

MAKES 8 SERVINGS

SHREDDED COCONUT

Sweetened shredded or flaked coconut is a moist form of dried coconut. It usually comes in a plastic bag, but it can also often be found in a can in the baking aisle of the supermarket. Toasting brings out the coconut's natural nutty flavor. To toast coconut, spread it on a baking sheet and toast in a preheated 350°F (180°C) oven until the edges are lightly golden brown, 8–10 minutes.

GRILLED PEACH MELBA

Preheat the oven to 325°F (165°C). Coat a 5-by-9-by-4-inch (13-by-23-by-10-cm) loaf pan with vegetable oil spray. Dust with flour, then tap out any excess.

To make the cake, in a bowl, mix together the flour, baking powder, and salt. Using a stand mixer fitted with the paddle attachment, beat the butter until pale and fluffy. Gradually add in the sugar and beat well. Add the eggs one at a time, beating well after each addition. Beat in half the flour mixture, then half the buttermilk, and repeat to add the remaining flour mixture and buttermilk.

Scrape the batter into the prepared pan. Bake until the center of the cake springs back when touched and a skewer inserted into it comes out clean, 40–45 minutes. Let cool in the pan on a rack for 15–20 minutes, then turn out of the pan and let the cake cool completely. Raise the oven temperature to 350°F (180°C).

While the cake is baking, prepare a charcoal or gas grill for direct grilling over high heat. Lightly oil the grill rack. Halve and pit the peaches, then cut each half in half again. Place the peach quarters cut side down on the grill rack and grill until marks appear, about 4 minutes. Turn them so that the other cut side faces down, and grill for another 4 minutes. Turn to place on their rounded sides and grill until the peaches sizzle slightly and are easily pierced with a skewer, about 4 minutes more. Transfer the peaches to a platter and let cool to room temperature. (This can also be done in a grill pan over high heat.)

Cut the cake into thick slices and arrange them on a baking sheet. Toast in the oven until the edges are a light golden brown, 8–10 minutes. To serve, place a warm cake slice on each plate and top with 4 grilled peach quarters and a scoop of the ice cream. Drizzle each serving with the raspberry purée and serve.

MAKES 4 SERVINGS

PEELING PEACHES

The easiest way to peel peaches and other thin-skinned fruits is to blanch them first. Score the blossom end (bottom) of each peach with an X. In small batches, immerse the peaches in boiling water just until the skins begin to wrinkle and curl at the X, 20–60 seconds, depending on the ripeness of the fruit. Immediately transfer the fruit to a bowl of ice water to stop the cooking. When the fruit is cool you should be able to slip off the skin with your fingers; use a paring knife to remove any skin that does not come away easily.

FOR THE BUTTERMILK POUND CAKE:

Vegetable oil spray

1½ cups (6 oz/185 g) cake (soft-wheat) flour, plus extra for dusting

1 teaspoon baking powder

½ teaspoon salt

½ cup (4 oz/125 g) unsalted butter, at room temperature

1 cup (8 oz/250 g) sugar

2 large eggs

½ cup (4 fl oz/125 ml) buttermilk

4 large, firm ripe peaches (about 1 lb/500 g total weight), peeled (far left)

Good-quality vanilla ice cream for serving

½ cup (4 fl oz/125 ml) Raspberry Purée (page 109) or purchased raspberry sauce for serving

CRISPS AND COBBLERS

The homey, comforting baked desserts in this chapter highlight the flavors of summer—berries, plums, peaches, and apricots— as well as the apples and pears of autumn. Whether crowned with a butter-rich cobbler dough or a crisp, crumbly topping, they can be perfect accompaniments to afternoon coffee or fine finishes for a casual brunch.

APRICOT-ALMOND CRISP

Place an oven rack in the lower third of the oven and preheat to 350°F (180°C). Grease a 12-inch (30-cm) oval or 9-by-13-inch (23-by-33-cm) rectangular baking dish with a 2-qt (2-l) capacity.

To make the topping, in a bowl, stir together the flour, oats, brown sugar, salt, ground ginger, and cinnamon. Using a pastry blender or 2 knives, quickly cut the butter into the flour mixture until it is crumbly (page 10). Add the sliced almonds and toss to mix. Cover and refrigerate while you prepare the filling.

To make the filling, in a small bowl, stir together the granulated sugar, tapioca, ginger, and salt. Place the apricots in a large bowl, sprinkle with the sugar mixture, and toss to distribute evenly. Spread the apricot mixture in the prepared baking dish. Sprinkle the topping evenly over the apricots.

Bake until the topping is crisp and golden brown and the apricot filling bubbles slowly, about 50 minutes. Serve warm.

MAKES 8 SERVINGS

THICKENING FRUIT DESSERTS

When fruit is baked, the flesh breaks down and the juices are released. These juices are an integral part of many desserts, as they contain a lot of flavor, but often they must be thickened so that the dish doesn't become soggy or liquidy. Both tapioca and cornstarch (cornflour) can be used to thicken fruit desserts. If you use quick-cooking (instant) tapioca for thickening, tiny, tender bits of tapioca will be visible, while cornstarch (cornflour) bakes up smooth.

FOR THE TOPPING:

½ cup (2½ oz/75 g) unbleached all-purpose (plain) flour

1 cup (3 oz/90 g) old-fashioned or quick-cooking rolled oats

½ cup (3½ oz/105 g) firmly packed brown sugar

¼ teaspoon salt

1 teaspoon ground ginger

½ teaspoon ground cinnamon

½ cup (4 oz/125 g) cold unsalted butter, cut into 6 pieces, plus extra for greasing

1 cup (4 oz/125 g) sliced almonds

FOR THE FILLING:

¾ cup (6 oz/185 g) granulated sugar

2 tablespoons quick-cooking tapioca or cornstarch (cornflour)

1 teaspoon peeled and grated fresh ginger

Pinch of salt

2½ lb (1.25 kg) apricots, pitted and diced

PEACH AND PISTACHIO COBBLER

FOR THE FILLING:

½ cup (4 oz/125 g) sugar

2 tablespoons cornstarch (cornflour)

½ teaspoon ground cinnamon

¼ teaspoon *each* ground nutmeg and salt

8–10 peaches, peeled if desired (page 40), pitted, and sliced 1 inch (2.5 cm) thick

FOR THE TOPPING:

2 cups (10 oz/315 g) unbleached all-purpose (plain) flour

½ cup (2 oz/60 g) unsalted pistachios, finely chopped

¼ cup (2 oz/60 g) sugar

½ teaspoon salt

2 teaspoons baking powder

¾ cup (6 oz/185 g) cold unsalted butter, cut into ½-inch (12-mm) cubes, plus extra for greasing

¾ cup (6 fl oz/180 ml) whole milk

Ground cinnamon and sugar for sprinkling

Place an oven rack in the lower third of the oven and preheat to 350°F (180°C). Grease a 12-inch (30-cm) oval or 9-by-13-inch (23-by-33-cm) rectangular baking dish with a 2-qt (2-l) capacity.

To make the filling, in a small bowl, stir together the sugar, cornstarch, cinnamon, nutmeg, and salt. Place the peaches in a large bowl, sprinkle with the sugar mixture, and toss to distribute evenly. Spread the peach mixture in the prepared baking dish and set aside while you prepare the topping.

To make the topping, in a large bowl, mix together the flour, pistachios, sugar, salt, and baking powder. Using a pastry blender or your fingers, cut or rub the butter into the flour mixture until the texture resembles coarse cornmeal, leaving some pieces of butter about the size of a small pea (page 10). Add the milk and stir just until the mixture pulls together. (Alternatively, this process can be done in a stand mixer fitted with the paddle.)

Pinch off chunks of the dough and place them on top of the peach mixture, covering it nearly completely. Alternatively, on a lightly floured work surface, roll out the dough to the same dimensions as the baking dish and carefully lay it over the filling.

In a small bowl, mix together ¼ teaspoon cinnamon and 1 tablespoon sugar and sprinkle the cinnamon sugar on top of the dough. Bake until the topping is firm and golden brown and the filling bubbles slowly, 45–60 minutes.

Remove from the oven and let cool for 30 minutes before serving.

Serving Tip: Accompany the cobbler with a small scoop of vanilla ice cream or a splash of heavy (double) cream.

MAKES 8 SERVINGS

PISTACHIOS

Unsalted raw pistachios can be found in well-stocked supermarkets and in most Middle Eastern markets and health-food stores. These bright green nuts have a mild flavor that complements the peaches without overpowering them. Pistachios and other nuts are rich in oil, which means that they can develop a rancid flavor if stored too long or improperly. Purchase nuts in small quantities as needed, and store them in a cool, dark cupboard or in the freezer.

SPICED BLUEBERRY COBBLER

Place an oven rack in the lower third of the oven and preheat to 350°F (180°C). Grease a 12-inch (30-cm) oval or 9-by-13-inch (23-by-33-cm) rectangular baking dish with a 2-qt (2-l) capacity.

To make the filling, in a bowl, combine the lemon zest and juice, blueberries, sugar, molasses, nutmeg, cloves, and cornstarch. Stir gently to mix, then spread in the prepared baking dish.

To make the topping, in a large bowl, mix together the flour, sugar, baking powder, and salt. Using a pastry blender or your fingers, cut or rub the butter into the flour mixture until the texture resembles coarse cornmeal, leaving some pieces of butter about the size of a small pea (page 10). In a small bowl, beat the egg and cream together, add to the flour mixture a little at a time and stir just until the mixture pulls together. (This process can be done in a stand mixer fitted with the paddle attachment.)

Pinch off chunks of the dough and place them on top of the prepared blueberry mixture, covering it nearly completely.

Bake the cobbler until the topping is firm and golden brown and the filling bubbles slowly, 45–55 minutes.

Let cool for about 45 minutes before serving with a small scoop of vanilla ice cream, if desired.

MAKES 8 SERVINGS

GRATING NUTMEG

Highly aromatic nutmeg, the hard brown pit of the fruit of the nutmeg tree, is one of the oldest cultivated spices. The seed's lacy outer covering, when dried and ground, is used as a separate spice called mace. Once nutmeg is grated, its volatile oils quickly begin to evaporate and its flavor diminishes. For the best flavor, buy whole nutmeg rather than ground, and grate it as needed using a specialized nutmeg grater, a fine rasp-style grater (such as a Microplane grater), or the smallest holes on a box grater.

FOR THE FILLING:

Finely grated zest and juice of 1 lemon

4 cups (1 lb/500 g) fresh or thawed frozen blueberries

½ cup (4 oz/125 g) sugar

¼ cup (3 oz/90 g) unsulphured light molasses

¼ teaspoon freshly grated nutmeg

¼ teaspoon ground cloves

2 tablespoons cornstarch (cornflour)

FOR THE TOPPING:

1 cup (5 oz/155 g) all-purpose (plain) flour

¼ cup (2 oz/60 g) sugar

1 teaspoon baking powder

¼ teaspoon salt

⅓ cup (3 oz/90 g) cold unsalted butter, cut into ½-inch (12-mm) cubes, plus extra for greasing

1 large egg

⅓ cup (3 fl oz/80 ml) heavy (double) cream

Good-quality vanilla ice cream for serving (optional)

CRANBERRY AND PEAR CRUMBLE

FOR THE TOPPING:

1½ cups (7½ oz/235 g)
unbleached all-purpose
(plain) flour

½ cup (4 oz/125 g) sugar

½ teaspoon ground
cinnamon

¼ teaspoon salt

½ cup (4 oz/125 g) cold
unsalted butter, cut into
¼-inch (6-mm) cubes,
plus extra for greasing

FOR THE FILLING:

⅔ cup (5 oz/155 g) sugar

Pinch of salt

2 tablespoons cornstarch
(cornflour)

6 firm but ripe Anjou
pears, peeled, halved,
cored, and diced (about
6 cups/1½ lb/750 g)

1 cup (4 oz/125 g) fresh
or unthawed frozen
cranberries, coarsely
chopped

Good-quality vanilla
or ginger ice cream or
Sweetened Whipped
Cream (page 17) for
serving

Place an oven rack in the lower third of the oven and preheat to 350°F (180°C). Grease a 12-inch (30-cm) oval or 9-by-13-inch (23-by-33-cm) rectangular baking dish with a 2-qt (2-l) capacity.

To make the topping, in a bowl, mix together the flour, sugar, cinnamon, and salt. Using a pastry blender or 2 knives, quickly cut the butter into the flour mixture until it is crumbly (page 10). Cover and refrigerate while you prepare the fruit.

To make the filling, in a small bowl, stir together the sugar, salt, and cornstarch. In another large bowl, combine the pears and the cranberries. Sprinkle with the sugar mixture and toss to distribute evenly. Spoon the fruit mixture into the prepared baking dish. Sprinkle the topping evenly over the fruit.

Bake the crumble until the topping is crisp and golden brown and the fruit filling bubbles slowly, 40–50 minutes. Serve warm with a scoop of ice cream or a dollop of whipped cream.

MAKES 8 SERVINGS

PEAR VARIETIES

Anjou and Bartlett pears are the best for baking because they remain firm and smooth when cooked. Anjou pears are almost egg-shaped, with green skin often tinged with yellow when the pear is ripe. Bartlett, or Williams', pears have thin skins that turn from dark green to light green and then to yellow as they ripen. When choosing pears for baking, select those that are firm but not rock hard, have a good fragrance, and are smooth and unblemished with stems still attached. Autumn is the best season for Anjou and Bartlett pears, but they are available almost all year long.

APPLE BROWN BETTY

MAKING BREAD CRUMBS

The bread crumbs in this dish absorb the butter and apple juices and begin to caramelize, giving the brown betty its marvelous texture. Choose a simple coarse bread with a firm texture; rustic Italian or French bread and sweet baguettes are good choices. Avoid breads that are rich in eggs or milk, as they will make the dessert mushy. To make bread crumbs, remove the crusts from slices of slightly stale bread (let the bread sit out overnight, or dry the slices in a low oven), chop coarsely, and use a food processor to reduce the pieces to coarse crumbs.

Place an oven rack in the lower third of the oven and preheat to 375°F (190°C). Lightly grease a 2-qt (2-l) soufflé dish.

Spread the bread crumbs on a baking sheet and toast in the oven until lightly golden, about 10 minutes. Let cool.

In a large bowl, stir together the granulated sugar, brown sugar, cinnamon, nutmeg, and the toasted bread crumbs. Add the apple slices and toss until the apples are well coated with the bread crumb mixture. Place one-third of the mixture in the prepared baking dish and dot with one-third of the butter. Repeat twice, finishing with the butter.

Bake until the apples are tender when pierced with a skewer or small knife and the bread crumbs are golden brown, 1–1¼ hours. Serve warm with a drizzle of cream.

Note: A betty is an old-fashioned dessert that has been traced back to Colonial times in the United States and may be English in origin.

MAKES 6-8 SERVINGS

3 cups (6 oz/185 g) coarse fresh bread crumbs *(far left)*

½ cup (4 oz/125 g) granulated sugar

½ cup (3½ oz/105 g) firmly packed light brown sugar

½ teaspoon ground cinnamon

½ teaspoon freshly grated nutmeg

6 firm, tart apples, peeled, halved, cored, and sliced very thin (about 6 cups/ 1½ lb/750 g)

½ cup (4 oz/125 g) unsalted butter, at room temperature, cut into small pieces, plus extra for greasing

Heavy (double) cream, at room temperature, for serving

PLUM BUCKLE

Vegetable oil spray

1½ cups (7½ oz/235 g) all-purpose (plain) flour

1 teaspoon baking powder

¼ teaspoon salt

1 cup (8 oz/250 g) unsalted butter, at room temperature

1 cup (8 oz/250 g) plus 1 tablespoon sugar

2 large eggs, at room temperature

6–8 plums (about 1 lb/ 500 g), halved, pitted, and each half cut into 4 slices

Ground cinnamon and sugar for sprinkling

Place an oven rack in the lower third of the oven and preheat to 350°F (180°C). Coat a 9-inch (23-cm) round or 8-inch (20-cm) square cake pan with vegetable oil spray. Line the bottom with parchment (baking) paper and coat the paper with more spray.

In a bowl, whisk together the flour, baking powder, and salt. In a stand mixer fitted with the paddle attachment, beat together the butter and the 1 cup sugar until pale and fluffy. Add the eggs one at a time, beating well after each addition. Add the flour mixture and mix well.

Scrape the batter into the prepared pan and spread evenly. Poke the plum slices into the batter, placing them close together. In a small bowl, combine ¼ teaspoon cinnamon and 1 tablespoon sugar, and sprinkle over the surface.

Bake until the top is golden, the edges pull away from the pan, and a skewer or cake tester inserted into the middle comes out clean, 50–60 minutes.

Let cool for about 30 minutes before serving.

Note: Another homey, old-fashioned dessert, a buckle is a dish in which cake batter is mixed with fruit, often blueberries, and then baked. It is often topped with a cinnamon streusel.

MAKES 8 SERVINGS

PLUM VARIETIES

Fresh plums are available from late spring through summer. You will find these juicy fruits in an assortment of colors, from yellow and green to deep pink, purple, and scarlet. Check the varieties available at your local farmers' market, and choose firm, fragrant fruits with sweet, tangy flesh, such as Simka, Santa Rosa, Seneca, or Satsuma.

PIES AND TARTS

Every season brings to mind a favorite fruit pie or tart. Summer calls for a fresh raspberry tart or hot blackberry turnovers, while autumn brings a craving for pumpkin pie or an old-fashioned pandowdy made with dried fruit. The new year begins the citrus season, when tarts filled with lemon curd make a cheerful and colorful addition to the winter table.

CHERRY PIE
58

BLACKBERRY TURNOVERS
61

PUMPKIN PIE
62

RUSTIC NECTARINE GALETTE
65

HARVEST FRUIT PANDOWDY PIE
66

LEMON CURD TARTLETS
69

RASPBERRY TART
70

CHERRY PIE

SOUR CHERRIES
There are two types of cherries: sweet and sour (tart). Sour cherries are grown in the north and midwestern United States. Because they have a very short season and need to be cooked before eating, most recipes call for processed and jarred sour cherries, which are convenient and readily available. If you prefer to make this pie with sweet cherries, substitute 4 cups (1½ lb/750 g) pitted fresh sweet cherries for the sour cherries, omit the cherry juice, reduce the amount of sugar to ¾ cup (6 oz/185 g), and add ½ teaspoon almond extract (essence).

Fold 1 dough round in half and carefully transfer to a 9-inch (23-cm) pie pan. Unfold and ease the dough into the pan without stretching, patting it firmly into the bottom and up the sides of the pan. Using kitchen scissors or a knife, trim the edge of the dough, leaving a ¾-inch (2-cm) overhang. Refrigerate the dough-lined pan and reserved dough round until ready to use.

In a small bowl, stir together the sugar, cornstarch, and salt. Place the cherries in a large bowl, sprinkle with the sugar mixture, and toss to distribute evenly. Add the vanilla and mix well. Immediately pour the cherry mixture into the dough-lined pie pan and dot with the butter.

Lay the second dough round on a lightly floured work surface and cut out a pattern of circles or other shapes with a small cookie cutter or paring knife. Save the cutouts for decorating the top. Fold the dough round in half and carefully position over half of the filled pie. Unfold the dough, then fold the edge of the top dough under the edge of the bottom dough. Crimp the edges with a fork or flute them decoratively (page 108). Apply the cutouts to the top dough, applying a dab of water to the bottom of each dot to help it stick. Refrigerate the pie until the dough is firm, at least 30 minutes. Preheat the oven to 425°F (220°C).

Bake the pie for 15 minutes, then reduce the temperature to 350°F (180°C) and bake until the crust is golden and the filling is thick and bubbling, 40–50 minutes longer. Let cool completely on a wire rack to set the filling. Warm the pie again before serving by reheating in a 350°F (180°C) oven for 10 minutes.

MAKES ONE 9-INCH (23-CM) PIE, OR 8 SERVINGS

Two rolled-out Basic Pie Dough rounds (page 110)

1 cup (8 oz/250 g) sugar

3 tablespoons cornstarch (cornflour)

¼ teaspoon salt

4 cups (1½ lb/750 g) drained jarred or canned pitted sour cherries, plus ⅓ cup (3 fl oz/80 ml) cherry liquid *(far left)*

1 teaspoon vanilla extract (essence)

1 tablespoon cold unsalted butter, cut into small pieces

BLACKBERRY TURNOVERS

1 cup (4 oz/125 g) fresh or thawed frozen black- berries, marionberries, or olallieberries

¼ cup (2 oz/60 g) sugar, plus extra for dusting

2 tablespoons cornstarch (cornflour)

Pinch of salt

1 sheet purchased frozen puff pastry, thawed according to package instructions (see Note

Line a baking sheet with parchment (baking) paper.

In a saucepan over low heat, combine the berries, 2 tablespoons water, sugar, cornstarch, and salt and heat, stirring constantly, until the mixture is thick and jamlike, about 5 minutes. Transfer the berries to a bowl and cover with plastic wrap, pressing the wrap directly onto the surface of the berries. Let cool completely in the refrigerator, about 1 hour.

On a lightly floured surface, roll out and/or cut the puff pastry as needed to make an even 10-by-10-inch (25-by-25-cm) square. With a sharp knife, trim ¹⁄₁₆ inch off each edge, and cut out 4 equal squares. Divide the filling evenly among the squares, placing about 2 tablespoons filling in the center of each square. Lightly brush the edges of each square with water and fold into a triangle. Gently press the edges together with the tines of a fork to seal. Place the turnovers on the prepared baking sheet about 2 inches (5 cm) apart and refrigerate for 15 minutes. Meanwhile, preheat the oven to 375°F (190°C).

Dust the tops of the turnovers with sugar. Bake the turnovers until puffed and golden brown, 25–35 minutes. Let cool for 20 minutes, then serve while still warm.

Note: The most common packaged puff pastry dough comes in a 17.3 oz (530 g) box containing two 9¾-by-9¼-inch (24-by-23-cm) sheets. Use one of the sheets to make this recipe, and save the other, well wrapped, in the freezer for another use. Or, double the filling and use both sheets to make 8 turnovers.

MAKES 4 TURNOVERS

WORKING WITH
PUFF PASTRY

Puff pastry, used in many sweet and savory French dishes, is made by layering butter within a pastry dough and repeatedly rolling and folding the dough. When the dough is baked, the butter melts and produces steam that causes the tender pastry to form many flaky layers. Using frozen puff pastry is a fine alternative to making homemade dough, which is labor-intensive. Thaw the dough in the refrigerator according to the package instructions, and keep it chilled until ready to use.

PUMPKIN PIE

FRESH PUMPKIN PURÉE
To make fresh pumpkin purée, first find a good baking pumpkin, such as Sugar Pie, Baby Bear, or Cheese. Split the pumpkin in half, leaving the seeds in place, and put the halves, cut side down, in a baking dish. Add water to a depth of ½ inch (12 mm). Bake at 350°F (180°C) until a knife easily pierces the pumpkin, about 45 minutes, adding water as needed to maintain the original level. When the pumpkin is cool, scoop out and discard the seeds, then scoop out the flesh. Purée in a food processor or blender until smooth. The purée freezes well for up to 3 months.

Fold the dough round in half and transfer to a 9-inch (23-cm) pie pan or dish. Unfold and ease into the pan without stretching, patting it firmly into the bottom and up the sides. Using kitchen scissors, trim the edge of the dough, leaving ¾ inch (2 cm) of overhang. Fold the overhang under itself and pinch to create a high edge on the pan's rim. Flute the edge decoratively (page 108). Refrigerate or freeze the shell until firm, about 30 minutes. Meanwhile, place an oven rack in the lower third of the oven and preheat to 375°F (190°C).

Line the pie shell with aluminum foil and cover the bottom with pie weights. Bake until the dough looks firm and dry, about 25 minutes. Remove the weights and foil and continue baking until just golden, 8–10 minutes more.

In a large bowl, whisk together the brown sugar and eggs until well blended. Add the salt, cinnamon, ginger, and cloves and mix well. Add the pumpkin purée and cream and whisk until smooth. Pour the pumpkin mixture into the dough-lined pie pan.

Bake until the filling has risen slightly and is firm in the center, 35–45 minutes. Transfer to a wire rack and let cool slightly. Serve warm with the whipped cream.

MAKES ONE 9-INCH (23-CM) PIE, OR 8 SERVINGS

One rolled-out Basic Pie Dough round (page 110)

1 cup (7 oz/220 g) firmly packed brown sugar

2 large eggs

½ teaspoon salt

½ teaspoon ground cinnamon

¼ teaspoon ground ginger

¼ teaspoon ground cloves

1 cup fresh pumpkin purée *(far left)* or prepared pumpkin purée

1 cup (8 fl oz/250 ml) heavy (double) cream

Sweetened Whipped Cream (page 17) for serving

RUSTIC NECTARINE GALETTE

One rolled-out Basic Pie Dough round (page 110)

¾ cup plus 1 tablespoon (4 oz/125 g) whole raw almonds, finely ground (page 22)

¼ cup (2 oz/60 g) plus 3 tablespoons sugar

½ teaspoon finely grated lemon zest

1 large egg yolk

4 large nectarines, about 1–1½ lb (500–750 g) total weight

1 tablespoon unsalted butter

Line a baking sheet with parchment (baking) paper. Fold the dough round in half and carefully transfer to the prepared baking sheet. Unfold the dough on the sheet.

In a small bowl, stir together the ground almonds, ¼ cup sugar, the lemon zest, and egg yolk. Spread the almond mixture into an 8-inch (20-cm) circle in the center of the dough.

Cut each nectarine in half and remove the pit. Thinly slice each nectarine half lengthwise, holding the half together as you cut. Use your fingers to fan out the slices slightly, and place them rounded (skin) side up, in the center of the almond mixture. Repeat with the remaining nectarine halves, arranging them around the first nectarine half and leaving a 1½-inch (4-cm) border of dough uncovered along the edge. Fold the edge of the dough up and over the nectarines, pleating the dough loosely all around the edge and leaving the galette uncovered in the center. Sprinkle the nectarines with the remaining 3 tablespoons sugar and dot with the butter. Refrigerate the galette until the dough is firm, at least 30 minutes.

Meanwhile, preheat the oven to 375°F (190°C). Bake the galette until the crust is golden brown and the nectarines are tender when pierced with a skewer or small knife, 45–50 minutes.

Let cool for 20 minutes before serving.

Note: A galette is simply a free-form tart, often made with plums or fresh figs.

MAKES ONE 9-INCH (23-CM) GALETTE, OR 6–8 SERVINGS

NECTARINES

Nectarines, a firmer cousin to the peach, have smooth yellow skin with red highlights. Select nectarines that are firm but not hard, fragrant, and free of blemishes. Nectarines continue to ripen when left at room temperature. If they give slightly when pressed, they are ready to eat; at this point they should be either used immediately or refrigerated and used within 5 days.

HARVEST FRUIT PANDOWDY PIE

Fold 1 dough round in half and carefully transfer it to a 9-inch (23-cm) pie pan. Unfold and ease the dough into the pan without stretching it, patting it firmly into the bottom and up the sides of the pan. Cover tightly with plastic wrap and refrigerate until the dough is firm, at least 30 minutes. Meanwhile, place an oven rack in the lower third of the oven and preheat to 375°F (190°C).

In a large bowl, stir together the apple slices, dried fruits, brown sugar, cinnamon, nutmeg, and salt. Pile the fruit mixture into the dough-lined pie pan. Dot with the butter. Lay the second dough circle on top of the fruit filling. Cut the top circle to fit inside the rim of the pan, about a 9-inch circle. Fold in the edge of the bottom dough, overlapping the edge of the top dough.

Sprinkle the top with the granulated sugar. Bake for 30 minutes. Reduce the heat to 350°F (180°C) and remove the pandowdy from the oven. With a small, sharp knife, cut a crosshatch of 1-inch (2.5-cm) squares into the top crust. Using the edge of a spatula, press the top crust down into the apples. Continue baking the pie, pressing the crust gently into the apples twice more during the remaining baking time, until the apples are tender when pierced with a skewer or small knife and the crust is golden brown, about 30 minutes longer.

Let cool to room temperature to set the filling. When ready to serve, heat in a 350°F (180°C) oven until warmed through, about 10 minutes.

Note: Typically, a pandowdy refers to a kind of deep-dish cobbler—sweetened sliced apples or other fruit topped with dough and baked. This variation uses a full pie crust, which is pushed down into the filling during baking so that it absorbs the delicious fruit juices.

MAKES ONE 9-INCH (23-CM) PANDOWDY, OR 8 SERVINGS

DRIED FRUIT

Removing the moisture from fruit concentrates its sweetness and flavor and results in fruit that is sticky, firm, and chewy. As dried fruit ages, its sugars can become crystallized; immersing the fruit in boiling water for a few minutes, however, will soften its texture. Golden raisins, Muscat raisins, apricots, peaches, sour cherries, prunes, and dried currants are all delicious choices for this pandowdy. Chopping dried fruit is made easier by first chilling the fruit in the freezer for 30 minutes.

Two rolled-out Basic Pie Dough rounds (page 110)

5 medium apples, peeled, halved, cored, and sliced ½ inch (12 mm) thick (about 5 cups/1¼ lb/625 g)

1½ cups (14 oz/440 g) mixed dried fruit such as apricots, peaches, currants, golden raisins (sultanas), and cherries, chopped if large

¾ cup (6 oz/185 g) firmly packed brown sugar

1 teaspoon ground cinnamon

½ teaspoon freshly grated nutmeg

¼ teaspoon salt

2 tablespoons cold unsalted butter, cut into ¼-inch (6-mm) cubes

1 tablespoon granulated sugar

LEMON CURD TARTLETS

Eight 6-inch (15-cm) rolled-out Basic Tart Dough rounds (doubled recipe, page 110)

FOR THE FILLING:

3 large whole eggs, plus 4 large egg yolks

1 cup (8 oz/250 g) sugar

2 tablespoons finely grated lemon zest

1 cup (8 fl oz/250 ml) fresh lemon juice (about 7 large lemons)

½ cup (4 oz/125 g) unsalted butter, cut into ¼-inch (6-mm) cubes

Transfer the dough rounds to eight 4-inch (10-cm) tart pans, easing them in without stretching them, and patting them firmly into the bottom and sides of the pans. Trim off any excess dough, and refrigerate or freeze until firm, at least 30 minutes. Meanwhile, preheat the oven to 375°F (190°C).

Line the inside of each dough-lined tart pan with foil, wrapping the foil up and over the edges of the tart pan to keep the sides of the dough from sagging. Cover the bottom of each foil-lined tart shell with pie weights and bake until the dough is set and lightly golden, 20–25 minutes. Remove the pie weights and foil and continue baking until the crust is completely golden, about 10 minutes more. Let cool completely before filling.

To make the filling, in a nonreactive saucepan over medium heat, combine the whole eggs, egg yolks, sugar, lemon zest and juice, and butter and heat, stirring constantly, until thickened to a puddinglike consistency, 12–15 minutes. Do not let the mixture boil. Remove from the heat and strain through a coarse-mesh sieve. Cover with plastic wrap, pressing the wrap directly onto the surface of the lemon curd. Refrigerate until chilled and set, about 3–4 hours.

Divide the curd evenly among the baked tart shells and smooth with a small spatula. Refrigerate to set the filling, and serve cool but not cold.

MAKES EIGHT 4-INCH (10-CM) TARTLETS, OR 8 SERVINGS

ZESTING AND JUICING
When a recipe calls for both citrus zest and juice, always zest the fruit first. If possible, use organic fruit for zesting. Whether the fruit is organic or conventionally grown, rinse it in warm water to remove any dirt, wax, or chemicals, then pat dry. Use a zester, vegetable peeler, or Microplane grater to remove just the thin, colored portion of the rind, being careful not to remove the bitter white pith underneath. To juice, slice the fruit in half crosswise. Working over a bowl, use a reamer or citrus juicer to extract the juice. Strain the juice before using to remove any seeds and pulp.

RASPBERRY TART

TEMPERING EGGS

To prevent eggs from curdling when they are added to a hot liquid, they must first be tempered, or heated in a gradual, controlled way. This is an important step when making custard (such as the pastry cream in this recipe) or any sauce that requires mixing uncooked eggs and a hot liquid. To temper eggs, beat them lightly until blended, then whisk in a little of the hot liquid to raise their temperature. Gradually add the remaining hot liquid while whisking constantly. At this point, the mixture can be returned to the stove for further cooking.

Fold the dough round in half and transfer to a 9½-inch (24-cm) tart pan with removable bottom. Unfold and ease into the pan, patting it firmly into the bottom and sides. Trim off any excess dough. Refrigerate or freeze for at least 30 minutes. Meanwhile, preheat the oven to 375°F (190°C).

Line the inside of the dough-lined tart pan with foil, wrapping the foil up and over the edge of the pan to keep the sides of the dough from sagging. Cover the bottom of the foil-lined tart shell with pie weights and bake until the dough is set and lightly golden, about 25 minutes. Remove the pie weights and foil and continue baking until the crust is completely golden, about 10–12 minutes longer. Let cool completely before filling.

To make the pastry cream, in a small nonreactive saucepan over medium heat, heat the milk just until tiny bubbles appear, 8–10 minutes. Meanwhile, in a medium bowl, whisk together the egg yolks and granulated sugar until pale yellow. Add the cornstarch and salt and whisk well. Gradually pour half of the hot milk into the yolk mixture while whisking constantly. Whisk in the remaining milk and pour the mixture into the saucepan. Cook over medium heat, stirring constantly, until the mixture thickens to a puddinglike consistency, 8–10 minutes. Do not let it scorch, and do not let it come to a boil. Scrape the custard into a bowl and whisk in the vanilla. Cover with plastic wrap, pressing the wrap directly onto the surface to prevent a skin from forming as it cools. Refrigerate until chilled, 2–3 hours.

To assemble the tart, whisk the chilled pastry cream until smooth. Add the framboise and mix well. Spoon the pastry cream into the tart shell and spread evenly. Arrange the raspberries, bottoms up, in concentric circles on top. Using a fine-mesh sieve, dust with confectioners' sugar. Unmold the tart and serve cool.

MAKES ONE 9½-INCH (24-CM) TART. OR 8 SERVINGS

1 rolled-out Basic Tart Dough round (page 110)

FOR THE PASTRY CREAM:

1½ cups (12 fl oz/375 ml) whole milk

4 large egg yolks

⅓ cup (3 oz/90 g) granulated sugar

3 tablespoons cornstarch (cornflour)

⅛ teaspoon salt

1 teaspoon vanilla extract (essence)

1 tablespoon framboise or other raspberry brandy (page 114)

3 cups (12 oz/375 g) raspberries

Confectioners' (icing) sugar for dusting

PUDDINGS AND FROZEN DESSERTS

Blending a distinctive fruit flavor such as lemon or strawberry with the silken texture of cream or milk creates a satisfying dessert. A lemon pudding cake served in a ramekin and a tangy lime mousse highlight the flavors of citrus, while a refreshing blackberry and Cabernet sorbet and zesty grapefruit granita make an impression without the use of dairy or eggs.

STEAMED PERSIMMON PUDDING

PERSIMMON VARIETIES
Fuyu and Hachiya are the most common persimmon types. The Fuyu is firm and crunchy when ripe, while the acorn-shaped Hachiya is quite soft. For this recipe, choose 2 bright orange Hachiya persimmons that have the stem and leaves still attached. Hachiya persimmons ripen after the first frost and are often sold rock hard. To hasten the ripening, place them in the freezer for 4 hours. As they thaw, they will become very soft. Cut away the top of the persimmon, scoop out the pulp, and whirl briefly in a food processor before pressing through a sieve with a wooden spoon to remove any fibers.

Choose a pot large enough to contain a 4-cup (1-qt/1-l) metal pudding mold with lid and a wire rack to hold the mold above the pan bottom. Place the rack and mold in the pan and add water to come halfway up the side of the mold. Remove the mold and bring the water to a boil. Coat the mold interior and lid with vegetable oil spray.

In a bowl, whisk together the flour, baking powder, salt, and spices and set aside. In a stand mixer fitted with the paddle attachment, beat the butter until fluffy. Add the sugar and beat well. Add the eggs one at a time, beating after each addition. Add the flour mixture and mix well. Add the persimmon pulp and beat until smooth. Spoon into the prepared mold and secure the lid.

Lower the filled mold onto the rack in the saucepan of boiling water. Return the water to a boil, then reduce the heat so that it simmers vigorously. Check the water every 15 or 20 minutes and add boiling water as needed to maintain the level halfway up the side of the pudding mold. After 1 hour and 45 minutes, check the pudding by removing it from the water bath, opening the lid, and touching the center. If it is firm to the touch, insert a skewer or cake tester; it should come out clean. If it is wet and sticky inside, return it to the saucepan and continue to check it every 15 minutes. The cooking time will vary depending on the shape of the mold and the depth of the saucepan.

Remove the mold from the saucepan and let cool on a wire rack for 20 minutes. Invert the pudding onto a flat serving platter and tap the mold gently to release it.

In a small saucepan over low heat, heat the jam until it liquefies. Pour through a fine-mesh sieve set over a small bowl. Using a pastry brush, brush the jam over the outside of the pudding to give it a gloss. Serve at room temperature with whipped cream.

MAKES 8 SERVINGS

Vegetable oil spray

1½ cups (7½ oz/235 g) unbleached all-purpose (plain) flour

1½ teaspoons baking powder

¼ teaspoon salt

¼ teaspoon freshly grated nutmeg

½ teaspoon ground ginger

¼ teaspoon ground cinnamon

½ cup (4 oz/125 g) unsalted butter, at room temperature

1½ cups (12 oz/375 g) sugar

2 large eggs

1–2 Hachiya persimmons, peeled and mashed to make ¾ cup (6 oz/185 g) pulp *(far left)*

2–3 tablespoons apricot jam

Sweetened Whipped Cream (page 17) for serving

LEMON PUDDING CAKES

½ cup (2½ oz/75 g) unbleached all-purpose (plain) flour

¼ teaspoon salt

3 large eggs, separated

1 cup (8 oz/250 g) sugar

1 teaspoon finely grated lemon zest

⅓ cup (3 fl oz/80 ml) fresh lemon juice (about 2 large lemons)

1⅓ cups (11 fl oz/330 ml) whole milk

Preheat the oven to 350°F (180°C). Place eight ½-cup (4–fl oz/125-ml) ramekins in a large baking dish and pour in water to reach halfway up the sides of the ramekins.

In a small bowl, stir together the flour and salt. In a separate nonreactive bowl, using an electric mixer on medium speed, beat the egg yolks with ¾ cup (6 oz/180 g) of the sugar until pale and thick, about 3 minutes. Stir in the flour mixture and beat until very thick, 2 minutes more. Stir in the lemon zest, juice, and milk.

Wash and thoroughly dry the beaters of the electric mixer. In a separate, clean bowl, using the mixer on high speed, whip the egg whites until foamy. Sprinkle in the remaining ¼ cup (2 oz/60 g) sugar and continue to whip until soft peaks form when the beaters are lifted. Using a rubber spatula, stir one-fourth of the egg whites into the lemon mixture, and then gently fold in the rest just until no streaks of egg white are visible. Spoon the mixture into the ramekins, dividing it evenly.

Bake until the centers are firm to the touch and lightly golden and the sides pull away slightly from the edges of the ramekins, 40–45 minutes. Remove from the oven but leave in the water bath for 15–20 minutes before lifting out the ramekins.

Serve these little pudding cakes warm or at room temperature straight from their ramekins. The top will be moist and cakelike, with a creamy pudding on the bottom.

MAKES 8 SERVINGS

WHIPPING EGG WHITES
Any trace of fat will prevent egg whites from whipping properly, so separate each egg carefully over an empty bowl to avoid getting any yolk into the whites, and carefully wash and dry the bowl and beaters to be used for whipping. To determine whether egg whites are sufficiently whipped, lift the beaters. Soft peaks will slump over to one side, while stiff peaks will stand upright. The eggs should still appear moist and satiny and not grainy— that is a sign of overwhipping.

FRESH LIME MOUSSE

Prepare four ½-cup (4–fl oz/125-ml) ramekins by wrapping each one with a parchment (baking) paper collar: Cut a length of parchment paper 2 inches (5 cm) longer than the circumference of a ramekin and at least 5 inches (13 cm) wide. Fold the paper in half lengthwise, wrap it around the outside of the dish so that it extends 2 inches above the rim, and secure with a rubber band.

Prepare an ice bath by partially filling a large bowl or the sink with cold water and ice cubes.

Pour ¼ cup (2 fl oz/60 ml) water into a saucepan and sprinkle with the gelatin. Let stand until the gelatin softens and swells, 5–10 minutes. Stir in the granulated sugar, salt, lime zest and juice, and egg yolks. Place over medium heat and cook, stirring constantly, until the mixture thickens and the gelatin melts completely, 6–8 minutes. Do not allow the mixture to boil. Set the saucepan in the ice bath until the mixture is cool to the touch. Remove the pan from the ice bath and let sit at room temperature while you whip the cream.

In a large bowl, combine the cream and the confectioners' sugar. Using a wire whisk or electric mixer on medium speed, beat until soft peaks form, 4–6 minutes. Add the lime mixture to the cream and, with a rubber spatula, fold together until smooth. Pour the mousse into the prepared ramekins, dividing it evenly.

Refrigerate the mousse until it is cold and firm, 2–3 hours. Remove it from the refrigerator 20 minutes before serving. To remove the collar, snip the rubber band and gently pull the parchment away from the mousse.

Note: This recipe contains egg yolks that may be only partially cooked; for more information, see page 114.

MAKES 4 SERVINGS

WORKING WITH GELATIN

Gelatin is an odorless, colorless, tasteless thickener derived from collagen, a protein extracted from the bones, cartilage, and tendons of animals. Two forms are available: powdered gelatin, popular with American cooks, and sheet or leaf gelatin, which is commonly used in Europe. Do not confuse powdered gelatin with the sweetened, fruit-flavored gelatin desserts sold in boxes. Both powdered and leaf gelatin must be rehydrated, or allowed to "bloom," in cool water and then melted before they can be added to a recipe.

2¼ teaspoons (1 package) unflavored powdered gelatin

1 cup (8 oz/250 g) granulated sugar

⅛ teaspoon salt

2 teaspoons finely grated lime zest

⅔ cup (5 fl oz/160 ml) fresh lime juice (about 8 limes)

4 large egg yolks

2 cups (16 fl oz/500 ml) heavy (double) cream

¼ cup (1 oz/30 g) confectioners' (icing) sugar

RUBY GRAPEFRUIT GRANITA

4 or 5 large fresh ruby grapefruits

⅔ cup (5 oz/155 g) sugar

Pinch of salt

Prepare an ice bath by partially filling a large bowl or the sink with cold water and ice cubes.

Grate 2 teaspoons zest from a grapefruit, then halve and juice all the grapefruits and remove the seeds from the juice. (It is not necessary to strain out the pulp.) Set the juice and zest aside in the refrigerator to chill.

In a nonreactive saucepan over medium heat, combine the sugar and 1 cup (8 fl oz/250 ml) water and bring to a boil, stirring to dissolve the sugar. Cook, stirring occasionally, for 2–3 minutes to thicken slightly. Remove from the heat and set the saucepan in the ice bath, stirring occasionally until cooled. Cover and refrigerate to chill thoroughly, about 4 hours or up to overnight.

In a bowl, combine the chilled sugar syrup, grapefruit juice and zest, and salt and mix well.

To freeze the granita, pour the chilled grapefruit mixture into a wide, shallow nonreactive baking pan or dish with a lid (or cover with freezer-weight plastic wrap). The grapefruit mixture should be no deeper than 1 inch (2.5 cm). Freeze the mixture until ice crystals form around the edges and bottom of the pan, about 2 hours. Using a fork, scrape the crystals from the edges and stir to distribute evenly. Continue freezing, scraping every hour, 3–4 times total. Finally, cover the granita and allow it to freeze overnight.

To serve, scrape the granita with a fork to separate the crystals, then spoon into chilled individual glasses.

MAKES 8 SERVINGS

ABOUT GRANITAS

Granita is the Italian term for an ice. Similar to sorbets in their vivid flavors, but with a more granular texture, granitas usually contain no dairy. Instead, they are made from a thin, flavorful liquid, such as fruit juice, wine, or coffee, and sugar. The mixture is placed in the freezer and stirred at regular intervals, rather than churned in an ice-cream maker. This method results in tiny icy crystals that melt easily on the tongue.

STRAWBERRY AND CRÈME FRAÎCHE ICE CREAM

Hull the strawberries (page 14) and coarsely chop them; you should have about 3 cups. In a blender, combine the strawberries, crème fraîche, cream, sugar, vanilla, and salt and purée until smooth. Cover and refrigerate to chill thoroughly, about 3 hours.

Pour the strawberry mixture into an ice-cream maker and freeze according to the manufacturer's instructions. Transfer the ice cream to an airtight container and freeze until firm, at least 4 hours or up to 2 days, before serving.

Serve accompanied with cookies.

Note: This Philadelphia-style ice cream—that is, an ice cream made without a custard base—relies on the fat in a cultured dairy product for its smooth texture and rich flavor. Do not use nonfat or low-fat sour cream for this recipe.

MAKES 1 QT (1 L), OR 6 SERVINGS

4 cups (1 lb/500 g) strawberries

2 cups (1 lb/500 g) crème fraîche or sour cream *(far left)*

1 cup (8 fl oz/250 ml) heavy (double) cream

1 cup (8 oz/250 g) sugar

1 teaspoon vanilla extract (essence)

Pinch of salt

Crisp butter cookies or tuiles for serving

CRÈME FRAÎCHE

Crème fraîche tastes similar to sour cream, which can be used in this recipe, but it has a subtler flavor. French and domestic brands are widely available, but it is also easy to make crème fraîche at home. In a small saucepan, combine 2 cups (16 fl oz/500 ml) non-ultrapasteurized heavy (double) cream with 2 tablespoons buttermilk and heat gently to lukewarm. Cover and let sit at warm room temperature until thickened to a yogurtlike consistency, 12–48 hours. The longer it sits, the thicker and tangier it will become. Refrigerate for 3–4 hours to chill before using.

BLACKBERRY CABERNET SORBET

1 cup (8 oz/250 g) sugar

1½ cups (12 fl oz/375 ml)
Cabernet Sauvignon or
other full-bodied red wine
such as Merlot or Zinfandel

2½ cups (10 oz/315 g)
fresh or thawed frozen
blackberries, plus extra
fresh blackberries for
optional garnish

Pinch of salt

Fresh mint sprigs for
garnish (optional)

Prepare an ice bath by partially filling a large bowl or the sink
with cold water and ice cubes.

In a nonreactive saucepan over medium heat, combine the sugar
and wine and bring to a boil, stirring to dissolve the sugar. Boil
until reduced to about ¾ cup (6 fl oz/180 ml), 10–15 minutes.
(Have a heat-resistant glass measuring pitcher handy to measure
the syrup and pour it back into the pan.) As the syrup thickens,
lower the heat to prevent it from bubbling over.

Remove the syrup from the heat and set the saucepan in the
ice bath, stirring occasionally until cooled. Cover and refrigerate
to chill thoroughly, about 4 hours or up to overnight.

In a food processor or blender, purée the blackberries until
smooth. You should have about 1½ cups (12 fl oz/375 ml) purée.
Strain through a medium-mesh sieve to remove the seeds. About
1 cup (8 fl oz/250 ml) purée should remain.

In a bowl, stir together the wine syrup, blackberry purée, and salt.
Pour the mixture into an ice-cream maker and freeze according to
the manufacturer's instructions. Transfer the sorbet to an airtight
container and freeze until firm, at least 4 hours or up to 2 days,
before serving.

Serve garnished with a berry or two and a mint sprig, if using.

MAKES 1 PINT (16 FL OZ/500 ML), OR 8 SERVINGS

MAKING SORBET

A sorbet is a fine-textured
frozen dessert that is similar
to ice cream, but is made
without any dairy products or
eggs. The churning action of
an ice-cream maker is what
gives a sorbet its smooth,
creamy texture. Alcohol can
inhibit the freezing of a sorbet,
but in this recipe most of the
alcohol is cooked off when
the wine is reduced to a
syrup. All that is left behind
is the full-bodied fruit flavor,
which marries well with
the blackberries.

BANANAS FOSTER

Peel the bananas. Cut each banana in half lengthwise, and then cut each half in half crosswise.

In a large frying pan over medium heat, melt the butter until it foams. Place the bananas in the pan, cut side down. Fry the bananas until they are slightly brown, 5–6 minutes. Turn them over. Sprinkle the bananas with the brown sugar and add the rum to the frying pan. Gently swirl to mix and continue to cook until the bananas are a deep golden brown, 4–5 minutes more.

To serve, place 3 banana pieces on each warmed dessert plate. Spoon the sauce in the pan over the bananas. Top each serving with a small scoop of ice cream.

MAKES 4 SERVINGS

3 ripe but still firm bananas

4 tablespoons (2 oz/60 g) unsalted butter

¼ cup (2 oz/60 g) firmly packed brown sugar

3 tablespoons rum

4 scoops good-quality vanilla ice cream

CARAMELIZING SUGAR

When sugar is cooked, it melts and develops a more complex flavor and deeper color. In this recipe, the sugar is mixed with butter for additional flavor and the butter-sugar mixture is cooked until it darkens. Be aware that cooked sugar becomes very hot and will badly burn fingers or tongues that venture a premature taste.

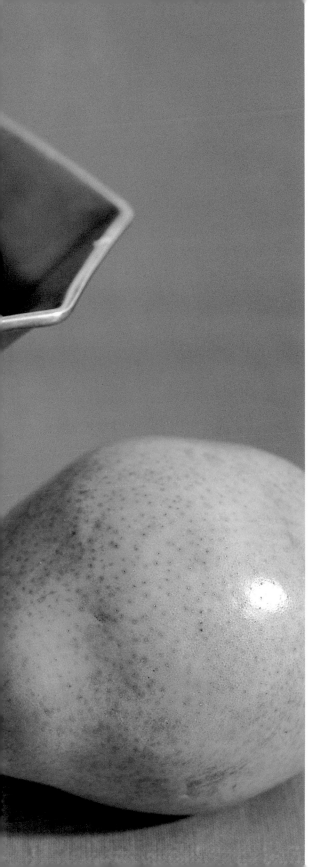

SPECIAL OCCASIONS

When a dinner party or other occasion calls for something out of the ordinary, these desserts fit the bill. A mixed-berry trifle will impress the most discriminating crowd, while a meringue-based plum Pavlova adds a refined touch to the end of a memorable meal. And for a formal occasion, nothing surpasses a glamorous soufflé flavored with Grand Marnier.

APPLE-BRANDY CRÊPES

CRÊPE-MAKING SAVVY

These thin, tender pancakes can be topped with sweet or savory ingredients after being folded. They are best made in a hot, well-seasoned crêpe pan, a flat-bottomed pan with sides that flare slightly. The first crêpe you make is "for the pan"; it won't turn out, but it allows you to determine the proper heat level for the pan (the batter should sizzle when it hits the pan). Use a flexible heatproof spatula to turn the crêpe after the edges are golden and the sides begin to curl; cook the second side briefly. Crêpes should be soft and flexible, never brittle.

To make the crêpes, in a blender, combine the milk, eggs, flour, oil, and salt. Blend until smooth, scraping down the sides once.

Heat an 8-inch (20-cm) crêpe pan or frying pan over medium heat until a drop of water flicked onto the surface sizzles. Wipe the surface of the pan with an oiled paper towel. Pour a small ladleful of batter into the pan and quickly swirl the pan just to cover the bottom with the batter. Cook until the crêpe no longer looks wet and the edges begin to curl and brown, about 1 minute. Using a flexible heatproof spatula, flip the crêpe. Cook for another 10–15 seconds, then slide the crêpe onto a plate. Repeat with the remaining batter, greasing the pan with an oiled paper towel as necessary. Let each crêpe cool briefly before stacking them on top of one another. You should have 8–10 crêpes. When the crêpes are cool, cover with plastic wrap and set aside until ready to use. The crêpes may be made up to 3 hours in advance and kept at room temperature, or refrigerated overnight.

In a 10-inch (25-cm) frying pan over medium heat, melt 2 table-spoons of the butter. When the butter begins to foam, add 2 tablespoons of the sugar and the apple slices. Sauté the apples until golden brown, 8–10 minutes. Transfer to a warmed bowl.

Fold each crêpe in half, then in half again to form a triangle. Return the pan to the heat and add another 2 tablespoons each butter and sugar. When the butter foams, place 4 of the folded crêpes in the pan and cook until they sizzle, 6 minutes. Gently turn them over with a spatula, remove the pan from the heat, and add 2 tablespoons of the Calvados. Return the pan to the heat and swirl to coat each crêpe well. Spoon 2 crêpes each onto 2 warmed dessert plates. Add the remaining 2 tablespoons each butter and sugar to the frying pan and repeat with the remaining crêpes, finishing with the Calvados. Serve warm with the apples on top.

MAKES 8–10 CRÊPES, OR 4 SERVINGS

FOR THE CRÊPES:

1 cup (8 fl oz/250 ml) whole milk

4 large eggs

1 cup (5 oz/155 g) unbleached all-purpose (plain) flour

2 tablespoons canola or safflower oil, plus extra for greasing

¼ teaspoon salt

6 tablespoons (3 oz/90 g) unsalted butter

6 tablespoons (3 oz/90 g) sugar

3 medium tart apples, peeled, halved, cored, and sliced lengthwise ¼ inch (6 mm) thick, about 3 cups (12 oz/375 g)

4 tablespoons Calvados or other apple brandy

SUMMER BERRY TRIFLE

2 cups (16 fl oz/500 ml)
Custard Sauce (page 109)

One 8-inch (20-cm) round
Yellow Sponge Cake
(page 109)

4 cups (1 lb/500 g) mixed
raspberries, blackberries,
and blueberries

2 cups (8 oz/250 g)
strawberries, hulled
(page 14) and sliced

½ cup (4 oz/125 g) plus
2 tablespoons sugar

1½ cups (12 fl oz/375 ml)
heavy (double) cream

1½ teaspoons vanilla
extract (essence)

2–3 tablespoons framboise
(far right) or Kirsch
(optional)

Prepare the custard sauce as directed and set aside. Bake the sponge cake as directed and let cool in the pan on a wire rack for 5–10 minutes, then cut into ½-inch (12-mm) cubes; you should have about 8 cups.

In a large bowl, toss together the mixed berries and strawberries. Sprinkle with the ½ cup sugar and toss to distribute evenly. Let stand for 15–20 minutes to create a syrup.

In a separate large bowl, combine the cream, the 2 tablespoons sugar, and the vanilla. Using a wire whisk, beat until soft peaks form when the whisk is lifted, 5–6 minutes. Cover and refrigerate until ready to assemble the trifle.

If using, stir the framboise to taste into the custard sauce.

Spread one-third of the cake cubes in a 3-qt (3-l) clear glass bowl. Spoon one-third of the custard sauce evenly on top of the cake, followed by one-third of the whipped cream, and one-third of the berries. Gently press the layers together, arranging the berries so that they can be seen through the glass bowl. Repeat the layering twice more, finishing with the berries. Cover the trifle with plastic wrap and refrigerate for 1–4 hours before serving.

Use a large spoon to scoop helpings of trifle onto serving plates or shallow bowls, and serve.

Note: Trifle, the quintessential English dessert, has an "everything but the kitchen sink" appeal. Here you get your cake, custard, and even your evening tipple all in one dish.

MAKES 8–10 SERVINGS

FRUIT BRANDIES
Fruit brandies, or eaux de-vie, are distilled liquors made from a variety of fruits. While the most common brandy is made with grapes, framboise is derived from raspberries, Kirsch from cherries, Poire Williams from pears, and Calvados, a specialty of the French region of Normandy, from apples. These brandies are not sweet, but instead reveal an intense fragrance and flavor of the fruit from which they are made. It often takes as many as 18 pounds (9 kilograms) of fruit to make a small bottle of eau-de-vie.

AUTUMN FRUIT STRUDEL

Place an oven rack in the lower third of the oven and preheat to 375°F (190°C). Line a baking sheet with parchment (baking) paper.

Working with 1 filo sheet at a time and keeping the others covered with a barely damp kitchen towel to prevent them from drying out, place the first sheet on the parchment paper. Using a pastry brush, brush well with some of the melted butter. Lay a second filo on top of the first and brush again with butter. Sprinkle with 1 teaspoon of the granulated sugar. Repeat, brushing every sheet with butter and sprinkling every other sheet with 1 teaspoon granulated sugar, until all of the filo is used.

In a large bowl, toss together the apples, brown sugar, cinnamon, nutmeg, and dried fruit. Arrange the apple filling along one long side of the filo stack, positioning it about 1 inch (2.5) from the edge. Fold the edge of the stack over the filling, then carefully roll up the filo into a log with the seam side down. Brush the log with additional melted butter and sprinkle with the remaining 1 teaspoon granulated sugar.

Bake the strudel until the filo is golden and the apples are tender when pierced with the tip of a knife, 45–55 minutes. Let cool on the pan on a wire rack for 30 minutes. Transfer to a long serving platter, cut crosswise, and serve warm.

MAKES 8 SERVINGS

WORKING WITH FILO
Filo (or phyllo) dough, best known for its use in Greek and Turkish pastries like baklava, is sold in the freezer section of large grocery stores. It is an elastic dough pulled into very thin sheets and cut into large rectangles. Follow the instructions on the box for thawing. When working with filo, keep the unused dough sheets stacked under a piece of plastic wrap or a barely damp kitchen towel until you are ready to use them; otherwise, they may become brittle and tear easily. Frozen filo dough keeps well, but not indefinitely; it becomes dry or sticky if stored for too long.

12 sheets filo dough, thawed if frozen

½ cup (4 oz/125 g) unsalted butter, melted and cooled

7 teaspoons granulated sugar

3 or 4 tart apples, peeled, halved, cored, and diced (about 3 cups/12 oz/375 g)

½ cup (3½ oz/105 g) firmly packed brown sugar

¼ teaspoon ground cinnamon

⅛ teaspoon freshly grated nutmeg

1 cup (7 oz/220 g) mixed chopped dried fruit such as sour cherries, apricots, cranberries, currants, golden raisins (sultanas), or nectarines

GRAND MARNIER SOUFFLÉ

1 cup (8 fl oz/250 ml)
Custard Sauce (page 109)

Unsalted butter for
greasing

½ cup (4 oz/125 g) plus
1–2 tablespoons sugar

¾ cup (6 fl oz/180 ml)
whole milk

2 large eggs, separated

¼ cup (1½ oz/45 g)
unbleached all-purpose
(plain) flour

Pinch of salt

2 teaspoons finely grated
orange zest

½ teaspoon vanilla
extract (essence)

¼ cup (2 fl oz/60 ml)
fresh orange juice

4–5 tablespoons
(2–2½ fl oz/60–75 ml)
Grand Marnier

½ teaspoon cream
of tartar

Prepare the custard sauce as directed. Cover with plastic wrap and chill in the refrigerator; bring to room temperature for 20 minutes before serving.

Preheat the oven to 400°F (200°C). Grease a 4-cup (1-qt/1-l) soufflé dish. Dust with 1–2 tablespoons sugar, tapping out the excess.

In a saucepan over medium heat, heat the milk until small bubbles appear around the edge of the pan. Remove from the heat. In a bowl, whisk together ¼ cup (2 oz/60 g) sugar and the egg yolks. Add the flour, salt, and orange zest and mix well. Slowly add half of the hot milk and stir until smooth. Add the rest of the milk, return to the saucepan, and cook over medium heat, stirring constantly, until the mixture is as thick as pudding, 5–8 minutes. Do not let it boil. Remove from the heat and stir in the vanilla, orange juice, and 2 tablespoons of the Grand Marnier. Cover with plastic wrap, pressing it directly on the surface (to prevent a skin from forming) and let cool for 15 minutes before proceeding.

In a small bowl, stir together the cream of tartar and remaining ¼ cup sugar. In a large bowl, using an electric mixer on high speed, whip the egg whites until foamy. Continue to whip while sprinkling in the sugar mixture until the whites are stiff, smooth, and shiny, 2–3 minutes.

Stir one-fourth of the egg whites into the cooled soufflé base to lighten it, then scrape the remaining egg whites on top. Using a rubber spatula, fold in the whites just until no white streaks are visible. Spoon the batter into the prepared soufflé dish.

Bake the soufflé until puffed and golden, 35–45 minutes. While it bakes, stir the remaining 2–3 tablespoons Grand Marnier into the custard sauce to taste. Serve immediately, drizzling each portion with the custard sauce.

MAKES 4 SERVINGS

SOUFFLÉ SAVVY

A soufflé is made from a light batter leavened by whipped egg whites. In the heat of the oven, the air in the egg white foam expands to make the soufflé rise. Soufflés should be served directly from the oven, before they have a chance to deflate. Soufflé dishes, made of ceramic to help hold in the heat, have tall, straight sides that are usually greased and then dusted with sugar (or, for savory soufflés, bread crumbs) to help the batter climb the sides of the dish.

ROLLED BLACKBERRY CAKE

ROLLED CAKES

ROLLED CAKES

This recipe calls for a thin rectangular sponge cake that is rolled into a cylinder while still warm from the oven, then cooled, unrolled, spread with a filling, and then rolled again. The cake is sliced crosswise when served, revealing a spiral design. These cakes are sometimes called jelly rolls—especially when they are spread with jelly as the first (or only) layer—or Swiss rolls.

Bake the sponge cake as directed and let cool in the pan on a wire rack for 5–10 minutes.

When the sponge cake is still warm to the touch, use a thin metal spatula or knife to loosen the edges from the pan. With a long side toward you, gently roll the cake into a cylinder with the parchment (baking) paper still attached to the bottom. Allow the cake to cool completely, about 45 minutes, then gently unroll it on a work surface and remove the parchment paper.

In a large bowl, combine the cream, vanilla, and confectioners' sugar. Using a wire whisk, beat until soft peaks form when the whisk is lifted, 5–7 minutes.

To assemble, spread the center of the cooled cake with whipped cream, scatter the berries on top of the cream, and reroll the cake. Transfer the log, seam side down, to a long serving platter. Cover with plastic wrap and refrigerate until well chilled, at least 1 hour and up 8 hours.

To serve, using a fine-mesh sieve or a sifter, dust the top of the cake with a generous coating of confectioners' sugar. Cut the cake crosswise into slices.

MAKES 4–6 SERVINGS

One 12-by-9-inch (30-by-23-cm) Yellow Sponge Cake (page 109), still warm from the oven

½ cup (4 fl oz/125 ml) heavy (double) cream, preferably not ultra-pasteurized

½ teaspoon vanilla extract (essence)

1 tablespoon confectioners' (icing) sugar, plus extra for dusting

1 cup (4 oz/125 g) blackberries

WARM PEAR CHARLOTTE

6–8 slices good-quality white bread or brioche, crusts removed

4–6 tablespoons (2–3 oz/ 60–90 g) unsalted butter, at room temperature

FOR THE FILLING:

⅔ cup (5 oz/155 g) sugar

1 teaspoon finely grated lemon zest

¼ teaspoon freshly grated nutmeg

1 pinch salt

4–5 ripe Anjou pears, peeled, halved, cored, and very thinly sliced (about 5 cups/1¼ lb/625 g)

1 tablespoon unsalted butter

Heavy (double) cream and/or good-quality prepared caramel sauce for serving

Place an oven rack in the lower third of the oven and preheat to 350°F (180°C). Have ready a 4-cup (1-qt/1-l) soufflé dish.

Generously butter the bread slices on one side. Cut all but 2 of the slices into pieces about 1½ by 3 inches (4 cm by 7.5 cm). Each piece should be no taller than the soufflé dish. Use the pieces to line the sides of the soufflé dish, placing them with the buttered side facing the dish and overlapping them by ½ inch (12 mm). Trim the remaining 2 bread slices into small triangles and overlap them on the bottom of the dish. Set aside.

To make the filling, in a small bowl, stir together the sugar, lemon zest, nutmeg, and salt. Place the pear slices in a large bowl, sprinkle with the sugar mixture, and toss to distribute evenly.

In a large frying pan over high heat, melt the butter. Add the pear mixture and cook, stirring gently with a wooden spoon, until the pears release their liquid and become tender, about 10 minutes. Remove from the heat and let cool briefly. Scrape the pear mixture into the bread-lined dish. (The filling can be piled higher than the bread, as it will shrink a little during baking.)

Bake the charlotte until the bread slices are golden, the pears are tender when poked with a skewer or small paring knife, and the juices are bubbling slowly around the edge, about 1 hour. Let cool in the dish on a rack for about 25 minutes.

With a small serrated knife, trim off any toasted bread edges that come above the rim. Run a table knife around the inside edge of the dish to release the bread, invert a platter on top of the dish, and then invert the dish and platter together. Lift off the dish. Serve the charlotte warm with the cream and/or caramel sauce drizzled on top.

MAKES 6 SERVINGS

ABOUT CHARLOTTES

Charlottes are molded desserts, served warm or cold. A standard charlotte mold is a pail-like tin with heart-shaped handles, but a soufflé dish or ramekin (for single servings) may also be used. The classic warm charlotte, lined with bread and filled with apples and custard, is transformed here into a pear dessert with a lighter filling.

PLUM PAVLOVA

Preheat the oven to 250°F (120°C). Line a rimmed baking sheet with parchment (baking) paper.

To make the meringues, in a stand mixer fitted with the whisk attachment, combine the egg whites, salt, and lemon juice. Beat on high speed until the large, foamy bubbles become small, about 2 minutes. Reduce the speed to low and gradually add the 1 cup sugar while continuing to beat. Return the mixer to high speed and beat until the whites are firm and glossy, about 8 minutes.

With a spring-loaded ice cream scoop or a large spoon, mound the meringue in 6 well-spaced mounds on the prepared baking sheet. With the back of a spoon, form a depression in the center of each mound. Bake the meringues for 1 hour, turn off the oven, and let the meringues remain in the oven for another hour. Remove from the oven and let cool to room temperature before serving. (The meringues may be stored in an airtight container at room temperature for up to 1 week.)

In a large, nonreactive sauté pan over medium heat, bring ½ cup (4 fl oz/125 ml) water and the ⅔ cup sugar to a boil, stirring to dissolve the sugar. Boil for 2 minutes to make a thin syrup. Add the plum slices and salt and return to a boil. Reduce the heat to a simmer and cook until the plums are tender, 3–4 minutes. Add the butter and swirl the mixture in the pan until the butter is melted.

Arrange the meringues on individual plates. Spoon the plums along with some of the juice on top of the meringues. Serve the Pavlovas at once.

MAKES 6 SERVINGS

FOR THE MERINGUES:

½ cup (4 fl oz/125 ml) egg whites (3–4 large eggs)

Pinch of salt

1 teaspoon fresh lemon juice

1 cup (8 oz/250 g) sugar

⅔ cup (5 oz/155 g) sugar

3 or 4 firm Simka or Santa Rosa plums, halved, pitted, and each half sliced into 8 slices

Pinch of salt

6 tablespoons (3 oz/90 g) unsalted butter, at room temperature, cut into ¼-inch (6-mm) cubes

BAKED MERINGUES
The original Pavlova dessert, a baked meringue topped with fruit and whipped cream, was named for the famous Russian ballerina Anna Pavlova. Making crisp meringues requires a high ratio of sugar to egg whites and a slow oven that will dry them out without giving them color. A gas oven with a pilot light is ideal for drying them out. Bakers seeking hard and completely dry baked meringues will leave them in the oven overnight to dry out. The Pavlova, however, calls for a softer baked meringue, crisp on the outside and slightly sticky on the inside.

FRUIT DESSERT BASICS

There is nothing better than a fully ripe peach that drips its sweet juice down your chin or a blackberry full of the complex flavors of the summer season. Each fruit has a flavor, texture, and aroma that is alluring and unique. Whether combined with nuts or liqueur, mixed into cakes or pies, or enriched with eggs and milk to make puddings or ice creams, fresh fruit makes a perfect ingredient for an astonishing array of desserts.

SELECTING FRUIT

Selecting ripe fruit that is in season is the first step in making great fruit desserts. Look for locally grown organic fruits at farmers' markets or produce markets. Talk to the farmer or produce buyer about the varieties available and ask for a sample when possible. Always look for fruit that has good color and, more important, a nice aroma. (Don't buy a melon that doesn't smell like melon, for example. If it has no smell, it is unripe.) Berries should have a deep color and be free of moisture, which quickly turns into mold. Stone fruits, such as apricots, nectarines, and peaches, should be firm but give a little when pressed at the stem end.

SEASONAL FRUIT

One way to ensure that you are using the best fruit on offer is to choose local, seasonal fruit whenever possible. The growing number of farmers' markets around the country, as well as an increased focus on local fruit in some supermarkets, has made the choices more abundant than ever. Here are some tips on what fruit is in season when, though bear in mind that different parts of the country have vastly different weather patterns and growing seasons. Fruit that comes into season in spring in warm climes may not be ready until summer in colder regions.

Spring is awaited with anticipation by cooks eager to start buying strawberries and other fragrant red berries. Cherries usually come to market in late May, followed by apricots, which continue into summer.

Summer brings a full range of favorite fruits, including peaches, plums, nectarines, melons, and bush berries (raspberries, blackberries, and blueberries). Strawberries linger, the second citrus harvest begins, and some apples make an early debut.

Fall brings with it crisp, cool weather, and on the heels of the first frost comes the harvest time for apples, pears, persimmons, and pumpkins. Baking can begin in earnest as the weather cools and we welcome the smell of spices and warmth from the oven.

Winter brings the true citrus harvest in January. Ruby grapefruit, Meyer and Eureka lemons, Key limes, Persian limes, and kumquats become increasingly available, and their tangy flavors are a welcome change to the chocolates, nuts, and spices enjoyed over the holidays.

SERVING FRUIT DESSERTS

The best accompaniments for a fruit dessert are often a simple dollop of whipped cream or a small scoop of ice cream. The flavor of any garnish accompanying a fruit dessert should be mild (such as vanilla or caramel) so that it highlights the fruit, rather than overwhelming it.

Baked desserts such as pies, crisps, and cobblers are often best when served slightly warm; be sure to warm the plates for the best results. Other desserts, such as puddings, are best if served cool but not cold. Allow them to stand at room temperature for 15 minutes before serving.

BAKING BASICS

The secret to good baking is starting with high-quality ingredients. Select well-known brand names instead of generic products for staples like flour, sugar, and vanilla. To accurately measure ingredients, use a glass or plastic measuring cup held at eye level for liquids and a set of nested dry-measure cups for flour and sugar. To measure flour accurately, stir it to aerate, spoon it into the measuring cup, and swipe the top of the cup level with the back of a knife.

CAKES

Cakes are leavened in part by beating or whisking the batter to create tiny air bubbles that expand in the oven. Butter-based cakes such as Plum Buckle (page 55) rely on creaming the butter for this physical leavening, while foam cakes such as the Yellow Sponge Cake (page 109) for Rolled Blackberry Cake and others rely on whipped egg whites. Sometimes a powdered leavener is also used to lighten the cake.

Cake batters can be made using a stand mixer fitted with the paddle attachment, a sturdy electric mixer, or even by hand, if you don't mind the workout. Cakes should be baked immediately after mixing for the best results. The cake pan should be greased with vegetable oil spray or butter, and the bottom lined with parchment (baking) paper.

Use an oven thermometer to check the accuracy of your oven, and do not open the oven door or jostle the cake while it is baking, which can cause it to sink in the middle. After baking, let the cake cool on a rack for 5–10 minutes before turning it out.

Slicing a cake into layers is best done with a long serrated knife. Place the cake on a plate and start the first cut one third of the way down from the top. First, rotate the cake as you make a cut 1–2 inches deep all the way around the circumference. Then rotate the cake a second time, this time cutting deeper into the layer with a slight sawing motion. Continue rotating the cake and cutting into the middle until you feel the layer release. Repeat the entire process, cutting the remaining larger section of the cake in half.

PIES AND TARTS

For the pie crust recipe in this book, butter is used instead of lard or shortening to make a crust that is both flavorful and tender. Select unsalted butter, unbleached all-purpose (plain) flour, and fine-grain rather than coarse salt when making both pie and tart crusts.

CUTTING IN BUTTER

Cutting butter into the flour mixture is an important step in making pie and tart dough. The butter-flour mixture should resemble coarse meal before the liquid is added. If the butter gets too warm the flour will absorb it and become sticky, resulting in a tough crust. To ensure success, start with butter cold from the refrigerator, work quickly, and, before adding the liquid, test the butter by giving it a quick pinch. If the small butter chunks are cold, your fingers will be grease free; if they are too soft, your fingers will be greasy. Should the butter become too soft, chill the mixture for 20–30 minutes before proceeding with the recipe.

Shown opposite are the basic steps in mixing pie dough:

1 **Combining the dry ingredients**: In a large bowl, using a whisk or a fork, stir together the flour, sugar, and salt.

2 **Cutting in the butter**: Using a pastry blender or two knives, cut the chilled butter into the flour mixture until the mixture is crumbly and the largest pieces of butter are the size of small peas.

3 **Mixing in the liquid**: Sprinkle 2–3 tablespoons water a little at a time over the flour mixture and mix with a fork just until the dough pulls together.

4 **Making the disk**: Gather the dough into a ball, then form into a disk shape.

ROLLING OUT DOUGH

To roll out pie or tart dough, on a lightly floured board, flatten the dough with 6 to 8 gentle taps of the rolling pin. Lift the dough and give it a quarter turn. Dust the top of the dough or the rolling pin with flour as needed. Begin rolling from the middle of the dough round, pushing outward and stopping the pressure ¼ inch (6 mm) from the edge so that the edge does not get too thin. Lift the dough, give it a quarter turn, and roll again. Use this frequent lifting and turning of the dough as an opportunity to gauge the dough thickness and to lightly dust the work surface and dough with flour to prevent sticking. Roll the dough out until it is about ⅛ inch (3 mm) thick.

CRIMPING AND FLUTING PIE CRUST

To crimp or flute the edge of a single-crust pie, pinch the edge of the dough between the index finger of your nondominant hand and the index finger and thumb of your dominant hand every 2–3 inches (5–7.5 cm) to form a scalloped edge. Or, with a thumb on top of the rim and a forefinger underneath, pinch together the dough edges, pressing the thumb down into the dough.

To crimp a double crust, first tuck about ½ inch (12 mm) of the top dough round under the bottom dough round. Dip a fork in flour and use the tines to gently press the layers of dough together, being careful not to poke holes in the top crust. To flute the edge, gently pinch the folded dough edge between the index finger of your nondominant hand and the index finger and thumb of your dominant hand every 2–3 inches (5–7.5 cm).

REMOVING A TART FROM THE PAN

To remove a tart from a pan with a removable bottom, set the tart pan on a wide can or coffee mug and guide the metal sides as they drop away from the bottom. Transfer the whole tart, including the metal bottom, to your serving platter. Gently slide the tart onto the platter and remove the metal bottom.

CRISPS AND COBBLERS

Crisps and cobblers are simple baked desserts that combine fruit with an easy topping. The topping for a crisp is typically a little sweeter and crunchier than a cobbler crust. A crisp usually contains brown sugar and another grain—often oats or cornmeal—in addition to flour. Crisps also often contain nuts, such as walnuts, pecans, or almonds.

Cobbler toppings, on the other hand, resemble sweet biscuits. Sometimes the dough is rolled flat and laid out into a smooth top crust, and at other times the dough is cut into decorative shapes. Most often chunks of dough are placed roughly onto the fruit before baking so the finished crust has a "cobbled" look.

CUSTARDS, PUDDINGS, AND FROZEN DESSERTS

Custards are egg-thickened milk or cream desserts that set with a silky smooth texture when baked or cooked on the stove top.

Puddings come in many forms. Some are smooth like custard, while others are more like a sticky cake. Whereas custards are usually set with eggs, puddings are generally thickened with cornstarch (cornflour) or gelatin. Puddings can be cooked on the stove top or baked in an oven, usually steamed in a water bath.

Ice creams usually consist of a cooked and cooled custard that is churned in an ice cream maker. Sorbets are frozen desserts based on a flavored sugar syrup; they are typically made with a fruit purée, which results in a creamy texture. Granitas are usually made with a juice or coffee, resulting in larger crystals that melt easily on the tongue.

BASIC RECIPES

The following basic recipes are referred to frequently throughout this book.

CUSTARD SAUCE

6 large egg yolks

¼ cup (2 oz/60 g) sugar

Pinch of salt

½ vanilla bean

2 cups (16 fl oz/500 ml) whole milk

Prepare an ice bath by partially filling a large bowl or the sink with cold water and ice cubes.

In a large bowl, whisk together the egg yolks, sugar, and salt. Set aside.

Split the vanilla bean lengthwise. In a heavy saucepan over medium-low heat, warm the milk. Using the tip of a knife, scrape the seeds from the vanilla bean into the milk. Add the bean pod to the milk and heat just until bubbles appear along the edges of the pan.

Gradually pour half of the hot milk into the yolk mixture while whisking constantly. Add the remaining hot milk and whisk until incorporated. Return the mixture to the saucepan and cook over medium heat, stirring constantly, until the sauce thickens and coats the back of a spoon, about 5 minutes. Do not allow the mixture to boil.

Set the saucepan in the ice bath until the mixture is cool. Strain the mixture through a medium-mesh sieve and chill well before serving. Makes 2 cups (16 fl oz/500 ml).

YELLOW SPONGE CAKE

Vegetable oil spray

½ cup (2 oz/60 g) cake (soft-wheat) flour

3 large eggs, separated

2 tablespoons unsalted butter, melted and slightly cooled

1 teaspoon vanilla extract (essence)

½ cup (4 oz/125 g) sugar

Preheat the oven to 350°F (180°C). Coat an 8-inch (20-cm) round cake pan or 12-by-9-inch (30-by-23-cm) jelly-roll pan (also called a quarter-sheet pan) with vegetable oil spray and line with parchment (baking) paper. Measure the cake flour into a sifter and set aside.

In a small bowl, mix together the egg yolks, melted butter, and vanilla. Set aside. In a large bowl, using an electric mixer on high speed, whip the egg whites until foamy. Slowly add in the sugar and continue whipping until the egg whites are stiff and shiny.

Pour the yolk and butter mixture into the egg whites and sift half of the flour on top. Using a rubber spatula, gently fold the ingredients together. Sift the remaining flour over the batter and fold in.

Scrape the batter into the pan and spread evenly. Bake until the cake is golden, the center springs back when lightly touched, and the edges are beginning to pull away from the pan, 20–25 minutes for the 8-inch round, and 7–9 minutes for the sheet pan. Makes one 8-inch (20-cm) round cake or 12-by-9-inch (30-by-23-cm) sheet cake.

RASPBERRY PURÉE

1½ cups (6 oz/185 g) raspberries

1 teaspoon fresh lemon juice

Pinch of salt

1–2 tablespoons sugar

In a food processor or blender, purée the raspberries until smooth. Add the lemon juice and salt. Add the sugar to taste and purée again until well blended. Strain into a bowl through a medium-mesh sieve to remove the seeds, pressing the mixture with the back of a spoon to push it through. Store in an airtight container in the refrigerator for up to 3 days. Let the purée come to room temperature for 30 minutes before serving. Makes about 1 cup (8 fl oz/250 ml).

Variation: Substitute coarsely chopped mango or coarsely chopped strawberries for the raspberries and proceed as directed.

BASIC PIE DOUGH

1¼ cups (6½ oz/200 g) unbleached all-purpose (plain) flour

1 tablespoon sugar

¼ teaspoon salt

½ cup (4 oz/125 g) cold unsalted butter, cut into ¼-inch (6-mm) cubes

3 tablespoons very cold water

To make the dough by hand, in a large bowl, stir together the flour, sugar, and salt. Using a pastry cutter or two knives, cut the butter into the flour mixture until the texture resembles coarse cornmeal, with butter pieces no larger than small peas. Add the water a little at a time and mix with a fork just until the dough pulls together.

To make the dough in a stand mixer fitted with the paddle attachment, stir together the flour, sugar, and salt in the mixer bowl. Add the butter and toss with a fork to coat with the flour mixture. Mix on medium-low speed until the texture resembles coarse cornmeal, with butter pieces no larger than small peas. Add the water and mix on low speed just until the dough pulls together.

Transfer the dough to a work surface, pat into a ball, and flatten into a disk. (Although many dough recipes call for chilling the dough at this point, this dough should be rolled out immediately for the best results.) Lightly flour the work surface, then flatten the disk with six to eight gentle taps of the rolling pin. Lift the dough and give it a quarter turn. Lightly dust the top of the dough or the rolling pin with flour as needed, then roll

out the dough, as described on page 108, into a round at least 12 inches (30 cm) in diameter and about ⅛ inch (3 mm) thick. Makes enough dough for one 9-inch (23-cm) single-crust pie or one 10-inch (25-cm) galette.

For a double-crust pie: Double the recipe, cut the dough in half, and pat each half into a round, flat disk. Roll out one disk into a 12-inch (30-cm) round as directed and line the pan or dish. Trim the edge of the dough, leaving a ½-inch (12-mm) overhang. Press any scraps trimmed from the first round into the bottom of the second disk. Roll out the second dough disk into a round at least 12 inches (30 cm) in diameter and about ⅛ inch (3 mm) thick and refrigerate until ready to use.

For a lattice-top pie: Double the recipe, cut the dough in half, and pat one half into a round, flat disk. Roll out the disk into a 12-inch (30-cm) round as directed and line the pan or dish. Trim the edge of the dough, leaving a ½-inch (12-mm) over-hang. Press any scraps trimmed from the first round into the bottom of the second dough disk. Pat the dough into a rectangle and roll out into a rectangular shape about ⅛ inch (3 mm) thick. Trim to cut out a 14-by-11-inch (35-by-28-cm) rectangle and refrigerate until ready to use.

Make-Ahead Tip: Pie dough may be made ahead and frozen for up to 2 months. To freeze, place the dough round on a 12-inch (30-cm) cardboard circle and wrap it well with plastic wrap. Alternatively, use the dough round to line a pie pan or dish, flute the edge, and wrap well.

BASIC TART DOUGH

1 large egg yolk

2 tablespoons very cold water

1 teaspoon vanilla extract (essence)

1¼ cups (6½ oz/200 g) unbleached all-purpose (plain) flour

⅓ cup (3 oz/90 g) sugar

¼ teaspoon salt

½ cup (4 oz/125 g) cold unsalted butter, cut into ¼-inch (6-mm) cubes

In a small bowl, stir together the egg yolk, water, and vanilla. Set aside.

To make the dough by hand, in a large bowl, stir together the flour, sugar, and salt. Using a pastry cutter or two knives, cut the butter into the flour mixture until the texture resembles coarse cornmeal, with butter pieces no larger than small peas. Add the egg mixture and mix with a fork just until the dough pulls together.

To make the dough in a stand mixer fitted with the paddle attachment, stir together the flour, sugar, and salt in the mixer bowl. Add the butter and toss with a fork to coat with the flour mixture. Mix on medium-low speed until the texture resembles coarse cornmeal, with butter pieces no larger than small peas. Add the egg mixture a little at a time and mix just until the dough pulls together.

Transfer the dough to a work surface, pat into a ball, and flatten into a disk. The dough may be used immediately or wrapped in plastic wrap and refrigerated until well chilled, about 30 minutes.

To roll out the dough, on a lightly floured board, flatten the disk with six to eight gentle taps of the rolling pin. Lift the dough and give it a quarter turn. Lightly dust the top of the dough or the rolling pin with flour as needed, then roll out as described on page 108 until the dough is about ⅛ inch (3 mm) thick. Use a small, sharp knife to cut out a round or rounds 2 inches (5 cm) greater in diameter than your tart or tartlet pans. If using a rectangular tart pan, cut out a rectangle 2 inches (5 cm) larger on all sides than the pan.

Makes enough dough for one 9½-inch (23-cm) tart or four 4-inch (10-cm) tartlets.

Make-Ahead Tip: Tart dough may be made ahead and frozen for up to 1 month. To freeze, place the dough round on a 12-inch (30-cm) cardboard circle and wrap it well with plastic wrap. Alternatively, use the dough round to line a tart pan and wrap well.

COCONUT ICE CREAM

1 fresh coconut or 1½ cups (6 oz/185 g) unsweetened shredded or flaked coconut

1½ cups (12 fl oz/375 ml) whole milk

4 egg yolks

⅔ cup (5 oz/155 g) sugar

Pinch of salt

1 cup (8 fl oz/250 ml) cold heavy (double) cream

¼ teaspoon vanilla extract (essence)

Preheat the oven to 350°F (180°C). If using fresh coconut, with an ice pick or screwdriver, pierce two of the three coconut "eyes" and drain out the coconut water. Place the coconut in a heavy-duty plastic bag and smash it against a concrete floor until the hard shell is cracked into ten to twelve pieces. Place these pieces on a baking sheet and bake until the coconut flesh releases from the shell, 8–10 minutes. Let cool. Remove the nutmeat from the shell and discard the shell. In a food processor or with a box grater, coarsely grate the coconut; you should have about 1½ cups (6 oz/185 g).

Prepare an ice bath by partially filling a large bowl or the sink with cold water and ice cubes.

In a saucepan over medium heat, combine the grated coconut with the milk. Heat until tiny bubbles appear around the edges. Turn off the heat and let stand for 30 minutes. Strain through a fine-mesh sieve and return to medium heat until bubbles appear around the edges, about 6 minutes. Meanwhile, in a large bowl, whisk together the egg yolks, sugar, and salt. When the milk is hot, remove from the heat and gradually pour half of it into the egg yolk mixture while whisking constantly. Add the remaining hot milk and whisk until incorporated. Return to medium heat and stir constantly until the mixture begins to thicken (it will read 175°F/ 80°C on a candy thermometer), about 6 minutes. Do not allow to boil. Remove from the heat and set the saucepan in the ice bath to cool the mixture completely. Stir in the cream and vanilla extract. Chill for 3–4 hours, then freeze in an ice-cream maker according to the manufacturer's instructions. Let the ice cream set in the freezer overnight before serving. Makes 1½ pints (24 fl oz/750 ml).

Note: Sometimes nature is unpredictable and even the most fragrant fruit can turn out bland. If the cooled coconut ice cream base seems to need a flavor boost, add ¼–½ teaspoon coconut extract to perk it up.

GLOSSARY

ALMONDS With their delicate flavor and smooth texture, almonds make an elegant complement to fruit desserts. To blanch and peel almonds, place the shelled nuts in a large heatproof bowl and pour boiling water over them. Let stand for about 1 minute, then drain the nuts in a colander and rinse with cold running water to cool. Squeeze each almond to slip it out of its skin.

BAKEWARE Different types of desserts require different types of bakeware. Below are some kinds called for in this book. (When in doubt about the size of a pan, fill it cup by cup with water to determine its volume.)

Baking pan: Baking pans can be made of glass, ceramic, or metal, and they come in many shapes and sizes. Foods bake more quickly in glass and ceramic dishes, so if a recipe has been written for a metal pan, you may need to reduce baking times and temperatures when using a glass or ceramic baking dish.

Baking sheet: A baking sheet is a rectangular metal pan with shallow, slightly sloping rims. It comes in several forms, including the half-sheet pan and the jelly-roll pan.

Cookie sheet: Cookie sheets are flat metal pans that usually have a low rim on one or two sides to allow for sliding cookies onto a cooling rack.

Ramekin: A ramekin is a small, usually round ceramic baking dish with straight sides. They come in many sizes, but 4, 6, and 8 oz are some of the most common. Ramekins are frequently used when making custards, puddings, and mousses.

Tart pan: Tart pans have shallow, usually fluted vertical sides. They come in a variety of sizes, but a 9½- or 10-inch (24- or 25-cm) diameter is standard. Look for one with a removable bottom, which allows you to free a tart easily from the pan.

BAKING POWDER VS. BAKING SODA Baking powder and soda are chemical leaveners. They work by reacting with both liquids and heat to release carbon dioxide gas, which causes a batter to rise as it cooks. Baking powder is a mixture of an acid and an alkaline, or base, that is activated when exposed to moisture or heat. Double-acting baking powder contains two acids. The first reacts when the batter is mixed, and the second reacts to heat during the baking process. Baking soda, also called bicarbonate of soda, is an alkaline, or base, that releases carbon dioxide only when in contact with an acidic ingredient, such as sour cream, buttermilk, or citrus juice.

BUTTER, UNSALTED Many cooks favor unsalted butter for two reasons: First, salt in butter adds to the total amount of salt in a recipe, which can interfere with the taste of the final dish. Second, unsalted butter is likely to be fresher, since salt acts as a preservative and prolongs shelf life. If you cannot find unsalted butter, salted butter will work in most recipes; just taste and adjust the salt in the recipe as needed.

COINTREAU An orange-flavored liqueur, Cointreau adds depth and flavor to drinks, desserts, and dessert sauces. Other orange liqueurs, such as Triple Sec or Grand Marnier, may be substituted.

CORNSTARCH Also called cornflour, cornstarch is a highly refined, silky powder ground from the endosperm of corn—the white heart of the kernel. It is used as a neutral-flavored thickening agent in fruit fillings, puddings, and glazes. Fillings and glazes thickened with cornstarch have a glossy sheen, unlike those thickened with flour, which are opaque. Recipes that call for cornstarch require additional cooking to eliminate any starchy taste.

CREAM, HEAVY Of all the dairy products, heavy cream has the most milk fat and the richest flavor. It contains between 36 and 40 percent fat. Heavy cream is also called double cream in Britain, and it may be labeled heavy whipping cream or just whipping cream in the United States. For the best flavor and volume for whipped cream, look for cream that has been pasteurized but not ultrapasteurized.

CREAM OF TARTAR This white powder is potassium tartrate, a by-product of wine making. It is used to stabilize egg whites so that they whip up more easily. Cream of tartar also inhibits sugar from crystallizing, adds creaminess to frosting, and contributes to whiter, finer crumbs and greater loft in cakes. It is also mixed with baking soda to create baking powder.

CRÊPE PAN This extremely shallow pan, with its flat base and sloping sides, comes in many sizes, but the most common is 9 inches (23 cm). The long, flat handle ensures ample leverage for flipping the crêpes, while the flat base and low sides make it easy to spread the batter in an even circle by rotating the pan.

CURD A thick, custardlike pie or tart filling made from eggs, curd is often flavored with the juice and zest of citrus fruit, usually lemon.

DOUBLE BOILER A double boiler is a set of two pans, one nested atop the other, with room for water to simmer in the bottom pan. Delicate foods such as chocolate and custards are placed in the top pan to heat them gently, or to melt them in the case of chocolate. The top pan should not touch the water beneath it, and the water should not be allowed to boil. A tight fit between the pans ensures that no water or steam can escape and mix with the ingredients in the top, which can cause melting chocolate to seize or stiffen. You can create your own double boiler by placing a heatproof mixing bowl or a slightly smaller saucepan over a larger one, although it may not be as steady or the fit as tight.

EGGS, RAW In some recipes in this book, eggs are left uncooked or partially cooked. These eggs run a risk of being infected with salmonella or other bacteria. This risk is of most concern to small children, older people, pregnant women, and anyone with a compromised immune system. If you have health and safety concerns, do not consume raw eggs.

EGGS, SEPARATING Eggs are easier to separate when cold. Carefully crack each egg and, holding it over a bowl, pass the yolk back and forth between the shell halves, letting the whites fall into the bowl. Carefully turn out the yolk into a separate bowl, and transfer the whites to a third bowl. Separate each additional egg over an empty bowl, for if any speck of yolk gets into the whites, they will not whip up properly. If a yolk breaks, save that egg for scrambled eggs or another use and start fresh with another egg.

EXTRACTS These concentrated flavorings made from plants are also called essences, and are often used to flavor sweet recipes. Extracts are made by distilling the essential oils of a plant and then suspending the oils in alcohol. Among the most common extracts used in baking are vanilla, almond, coconut, anise, and mint. When possible, choose pure extracts over imitation flavorings, which rely on synthetic compounds and have a less complex flavor. Store extracts in a cool, dark place for up to 1 year.

FLOUR
All-Purpose: Also known as plain flour, all-purpose flour is a popular general-use flour that is good for a wide range of desserts. It is made from a mixture of soft and hard wheats.

Cake: Low in protein and high in starch, cake flour is milled from soft wheat and contains cornstarch. It is very fine in texture and has also undergone a bleaching process that increases its ability to hold water and sugar. Cakes made with cake flour are lighter and finer in texture.

FOLDING This technique is used to blend two mixtures (or ingredients) of different densities without losing volume or loft. To fold, spoon some of the lighter mixture (often beaten egg whites) into the heavier mixture and, using a rubber spatula, cut down through both of the mixtures to the bottom of the bowl. Using a circular motion, bring the spatula up along the side of the bowl farthest from you, lifting up some of the mixture from the bottom of the bowl and "folding" it over the top one. Rotate the bowl a quarter turn and repeat just until both mixtures have been blended.

FRAMBOISE This clear brandy made from raspberries originates in the Alsace region of France. It is available at most supermarkets.

GRAND MARNIER Grand Marnier is the grande dame of orange-flavored liqueurs, which also include Cointreau, curaçao, and Triple Sec. Grand Marnier is made by flavoring brandy with bitter Haitian orange peel, vanilla, and spices. It is typically sipped over ice when not being used—always sparingly—in desserts and dessert sauces.

ICE-CREAM MAKERS Most ice cream and sorbet recipes require the use of an ice-cream maker that contains a canister and a churn. Not all ice-cream makers are the same: The more traditional kind requires the use of ice and rock salt, but most contemporary ice-cream makers use a frozen or refrigerated canister instead. Refer to the manufacturer's instructions for how to use your particular machine.

MELON BALLER Also known as a vegetable scoop, potato baller, or melon-ball scoop, this handy tool has a small bowl at one end, usually about 1 inch (2.5 cm) in diameter, used for making decorative balls from melon or other semifirm foods. It is also useful for seeding or coring apples and pears.

NONREACTIVE Selecting cookware made from a nonreactive material such as stainless steel, enamel, or glass is important when cooking with acidic ingredients such as citrus juice, or when cooking eggs. Cookware made with materials such as aluminum and, to a lesser degree, cast iron, will react with acidic ingredients and with the hydrogen sulfide in eggs; it can impart a metallic taste and grayish color. (Unlined copper has a desirable reaction with eggs, making egg whites more stable when they are whipped into a foam.)

NUTS, TOASTING Toasting nuts will intensify their flavor and give them a crisp texture and attractive golden color. To toast nuts, spread them in a single layer on a baking sheet and bake them in a 325°F (165°C) oven, stirring or shaking them occasionally to prevent burning, until the nuts are golden and fragrant. Depending on the type of nut and size of the pieces, this will take 10 to 20 minutes. Remove the nuts from the pan as soon as they start to brown and transfer to a plate to cool. Or, toast nuts in a small, dry frying pan over medium heat. Shake the pan often, and remove the nuts when they start to brown.

PIE WEIGHTS Also known as pastry weights, these small aluminum or ceramic pellets are used, along with aluminum foil or parchment (baking) paper, to weigh down pastry dough while it bakes, preventing it from puffing up in the middle. Raw short-grain rice

will work in their place, as will dried beans—though, when heated, these can give off an unpleasant odor.

SUGAR
Brown: Rich in flavor, brown sugar is granulated sugar colored with molasses. It has a soft, moist texture and comes in mild-flavored light brown and strong-flavored dark brown varieties. Either of these types will work in the recipes in this book.

Confectioners': Also called powdered or icing sugar, confectioners' sugar is granulated sugar that has been crushed to a powder and mixed with a little cornstarch (cornflour).

Granulated: The most common sugar is granulated white sugar, which has been extracted from sugarcane or beets and refined by boiling, centrifuging, chemical treatment, and straining. For baking recipes, buy only sugar that is labeled *cane sugar;* beet sugar may have an unpredictable effect.

Superfine: When finely ground, granulated sugar becomes superfine sugar, also known as caster sugar. Because it dissolves rapidly, it is preferred for delicate mixtures such as beaten egg whites. To make your own, process granulated sugar in a food processor.

VEGETABLE OIL SPRAY A boon to the baker, canola and other vegetable oils are available in spray cans that allow for quick coating of a cake pan. Regular oil or butter may be substituted.

INDEX

SIMON & SCHUSTER SOURCE
A division of Simon & Schuster, Inc.
Rockefeller Center
1230 Avenue of the Americas
New York, NY 10020

WILLIAMS-SONOMA
Founder and Vice-Chairman: Chuck Williams

WELDON OWEN INC.
Chief Executive Officer: John Owen
President and Chief Operating Officer: Terry Newell
Vice President, International Sales: Stuart Laurence
Creative Director: Gaye Allen
Series Editor: Sarah Putman Clegg
Editor: Emily Miller
Designer: Marisa Kwek
Production Director: Chris Hemesath
Color Manager: Teri Bell
Shipping and Production Coordinator: Todd Rechner

Weldon Owen wishes to thank the
following people for their generous assistance
and support in producing this book: Copy Editor
Sharron Wood; Contributing Editor Sharon Silva;
Food and Prop Stylists Kim Konecny and Erin Quon;
Photographer's Assistant Faiza Ali; Proofreaders Arin
Hailey and Carrie Bradley; Indexer Ken Della Penta;
Recipe Tester Peggy Fallon.

Set in Trajan, Utopia, and Vectora.

A Weldon Owen Production

For information regarding special discounts for
bulk purchases, contact Simon & Schuster Special
Sales at 1-800-456-6798 or
business@simonandschuster.com

Color separations by Bright Arts Graphics
Singapore (Pte.) Ltd. Printed and bound in
Singapore by Tien Wah Press (Pte.) Ltd.

First printed in 2004.

10 9 8 7 6 5 4 3

Library of Congress Cataloging-in-Publication Data

Weil, Carolyn Beth, 1958-
Fruit dessert / recipes and text, Carolyn Beth Weil;
general editor, Chuck Williams; photographs,
Maren Caruso.
p. cm. Includes index
1. Desserts. 2. Cookery (Fruit) I. Title: At head of
title: Williams-Sonoma.II Title: Williams-Sonoma
fruit dessert. III. Williams, Chuck. IV. Title.
TX773. W426 2005
641.8'6-dc22

ISBN 13: 978-0-7432-6189-0

A NOTE ON WEIGHTS AND MEASURES

All recipes include customary U.S. and metric measurements. Metric conversions are based on
a standard developed for these books and have been rounded off. Actual weights may vary.